Level C
Contents

BASIC Phonics Skills

Reproducible Skill Sheets

Choose from a number of reproducibles to practice each skill.
Skill sheets present varying levels of difficulty to meet individual student needs.

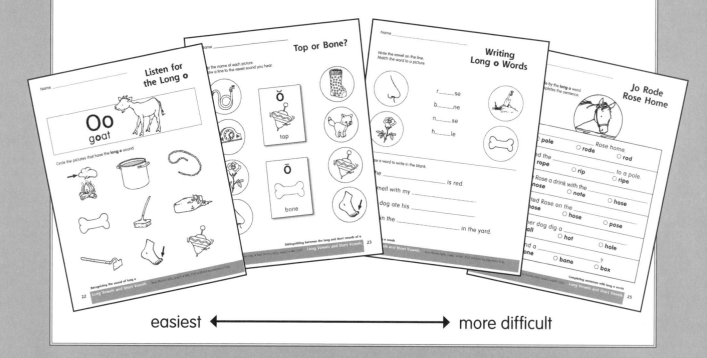

easiest ◀━━━━━━━━━━━━━━━━━━━━▶ more difficult

Review provided in each skill section.

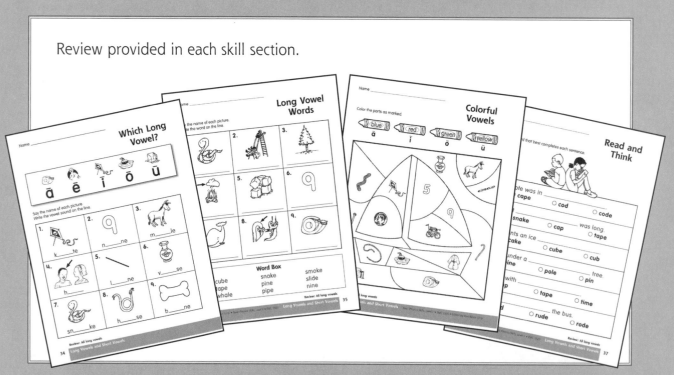

Word Family Sliders and Skill Sheets

Word Family Sliders provide repeat practice of major word families.

Activity sheets reinforce word families presented on the sliders.

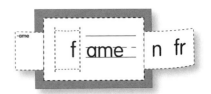

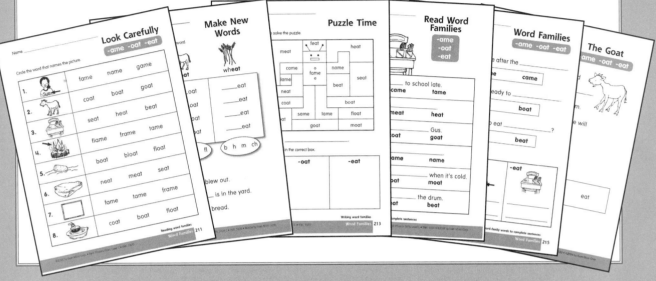

Little Phonics Readers

8 long vowel readers

12 word family readers

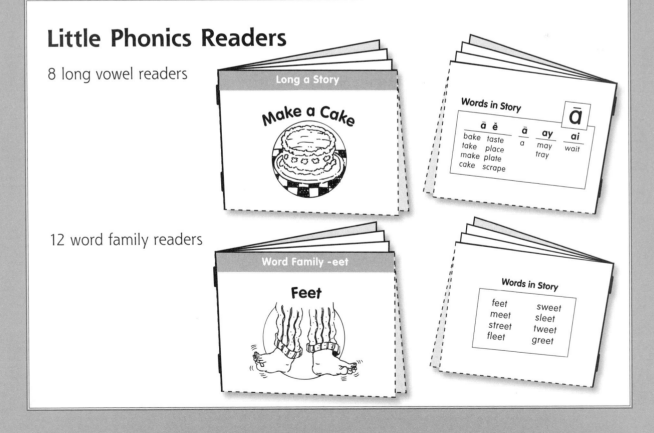

Tracking Student Progress

Use the form on page 5 to record the progress of each student. The rubric below will help you assess each student's level of competence. Students who fail to achieve a 2 or 3 level should be provided with additional instruction and practice until they become proficient.

Mastered **3**	• The student is able to complete the activity independently. • The student is able to complete the activity correctly. • The student is able to answer questions about the phonetic principle being practiced.
Showed Adequate Understanding **2**	• The student is able to complete the activity with little assistance. • The student is able to complete the activity with minimal errors. • The student is able to answer some questions about the phonetic principle being practiced.
Showed Inconsistent Understanding **1**	• The student required assistance to complete the activity. • The student made several errors. • The student did not appear to understand the phonetic principle being practiced.
Showed Little or No Understanding **0**	• The student required one-to-one assistance to complete the activity, or was unable to complete the activity. • The student made many errors. • The student showed no understanding of the phonetic principle being practiced.

Basic Phonics Skills, Level C
Student Record Form

Name _____

Sound or Skill Practiced	Level C Page Number	Date Completed	3 Mastered	2 Showed Adequate Understanding	1 Showed Inconsistent Understanding	0 Showed Little or No Understanding

The Benefits of Phonics Instruction

Words are made of letters, and letters stand for sounds. That is the simple basis for providing phonics instruction to all beginning readers. Research has shown that all children will benefit from being taught the sound-spelling connection of the English language (Chall, 1967). Phonics instruction leads to decoding, which gives beginning readers one more strategy to use when faced with an unfamiliar word.

Research has shown the following to be true:

- Strong decoding skills in early readers correlate highly with future success in reading comprehension (Beck and Juel, 1995).

- As more and more "sounded-out" words become sight words, readers have more time to devote to the real reason for reading: making meaning from print (LaBerge and Samuels, 1974; Freedman and Calfee, 1984).

- Readers who are good decoders read more words than those who are poor decoders (Juel, 1988).

- Children with limited learning opportunities and abilities benefit most from phonics instruction, but more able children also benefit (Chall, 1967).

- Those who are successful decoders do not depend on context clues as much as those who are poor decoders (Gough and Juel, 1991).

The best readers can decode words. As a result, those readers grow in word recognition, fluency, automaticity, and comprehension. "Sounding out" unfamiliar words is a skill that benefits all readers. These new words quickly become "sight words," those recognized immediately in text, which allow the reader to spend more time on new words. This cycle is the foundation that creates reading success, and successful readers are better learners.

Basic Phonics Skills, Level C • EMC 3320 • ©2004 by Evan-Moor Corp.

Long Vowels and Short Vowels

BASIC Phonics Skills

Note: Reproduce this chart on an overhead transparency to use as you review short vowels and present long vowel sounds.

Vowels

Vowels are letters.

a e i o u

Each vowel can be short or long.

Short Vowels		Long Vowels	
ă	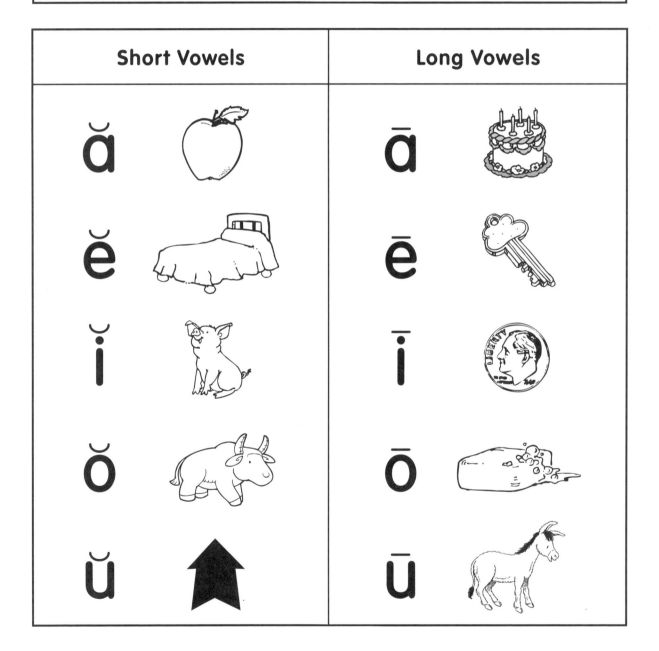	ā	
ĕ		ē	
ĭ		ī	
ŏ		ō	
ŭ		ū	

Recognizing long and short vowel sounds

Aa
cake

Circle the pictures that have the **long a** sound.

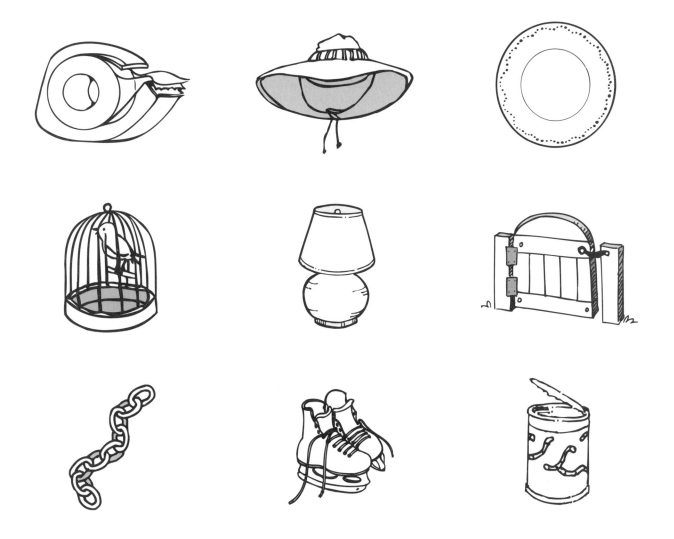

Name _____

Apple or Ape?

Say the name of each picture.
Draw a line to the vowel sound you hear.

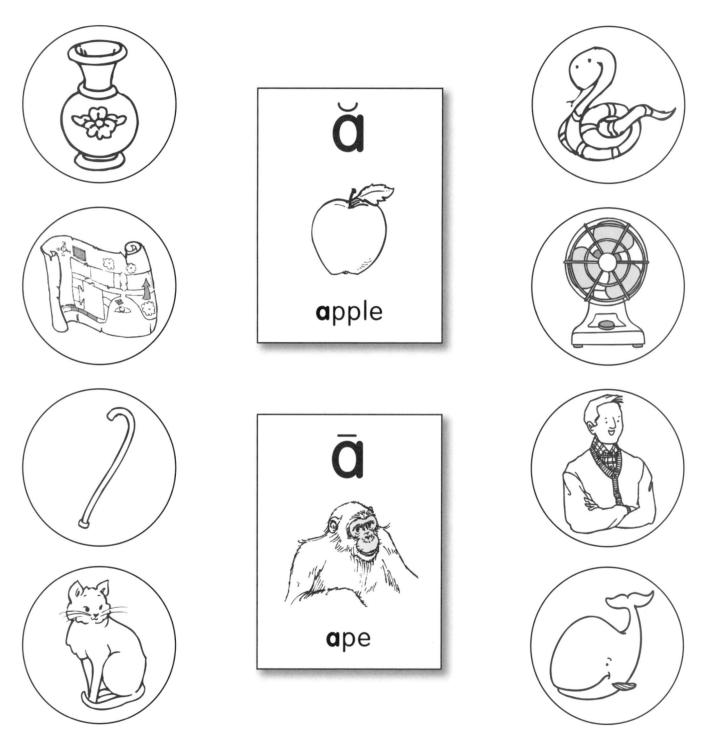

ă

apple

ā

ape

Name _____

Write the vowel on the line.
Match the word to a picture.

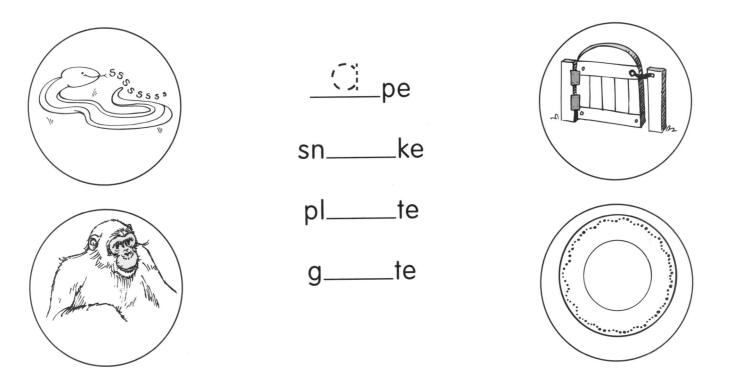

_____pe

sn_____ke

pl_____te

g_____te

_____

Choose a word to write in the blank.

1. Put the cake on a _____.

2. The green _____ ate fast.

3. Shut the back _____.

4. The _____ sat in a tree.

Name _____

Jake's Snake

Fill in the circle by the **long a** word that completes the sentence.

1. Jake had a pet _____.
   ○ **snake**   ○ **snac**   ○ **cane**

2. He fed it on a _____.
   ○ **tape**   ○ **came**   ○ **plate**

3. Jake did not shut the _____.
   ○ **game**   ○ **gate**   ○ **cake**

4. The snake left its _____.
   ○ **cage**   ○ **cake**   ○ **can**

5. The snake hid in that _____.
   ○ **gate**   ○ **same**   ○ **vase**

6. Will _____ find his snake?
   ○ **Jill**   ○ **Jack**   ○ **Jake**

Completing sentences with long **a** words

Long Vowels and Short Vowels   Basic Phonics Skills, Level C • EMC 3320 • ©2004 by Evan-Moor Corp.

Name _____

Note: Identify the pictures of he, we, and she for students.

me

Circle the pictures that have the **long e** sound.

Recognizing the sound of long e

Name _____

Jet or Me?

Say the name of each picture.
Draw a line to the vowel sound you hear.

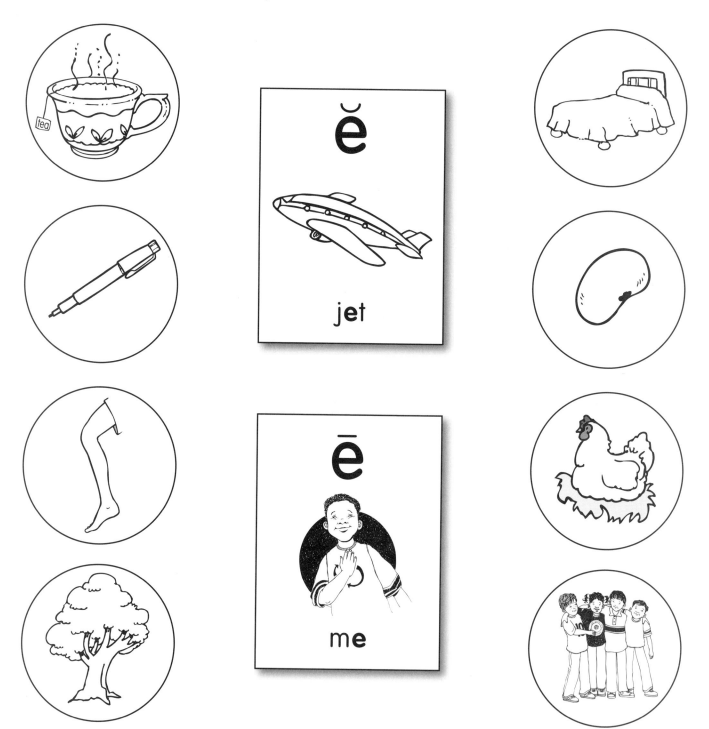

ĕ

jet

ē

me

Name _____

we   tree

Write the letters on the lines.

e	**ee**
h_____	b_____
sh_____	L_____
b_____	s_____

Write one of the words above in each blank.

1. I can _____ the tree.

2. The _____ can buzz.

3. I will _____ late today.

Name _____

Bees Buzz

Fill in the circle by the **long e** word that best completes the sentence.

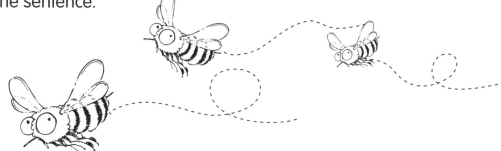

1. Lee is in a _____.
- ○ **she**
- ○ **tree**
- ○ **bee**

2. _____ bees are in the tree.
- ○ **Three**
- ○ **Lee**
- ○ **Be**

3. Can Lee _____ the bees?
- ○ **she**
- ○ **seed**
- ○ **see**

4. The _____ buzz.
- ○ **cats**
- ○ **bees**
- ○ **snakes**

5. _____ did see the bees.
- ○ **Lee**
- ○ **Be**
- ○ **Me**

6. Will Lee _____?
- ○ **bee**
- ○ **flee**
- ○ **seed**

Completing sentences with long **e** words

Long Vowels and Short Vowels Basic Phonics Skills, Level C • EMC 3320 • ©2004 by Evan-Moor Corp.

Name _____

Color the Shapes

Color the parts as marked.

long ē   short ĕ   long ā   short ă

brown   green   blue   yellow

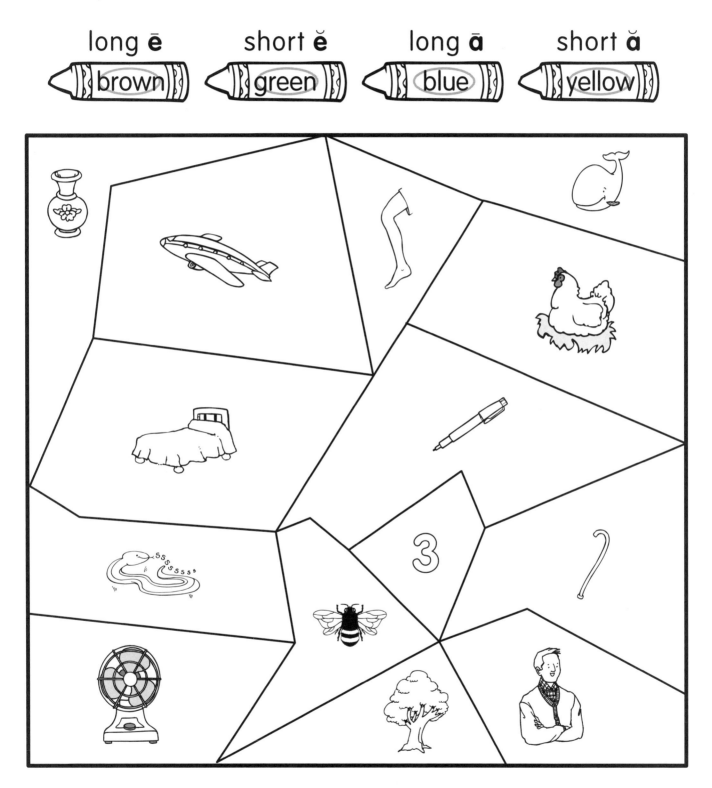

Distinguishing between vowel sounds

Listen for the Long i

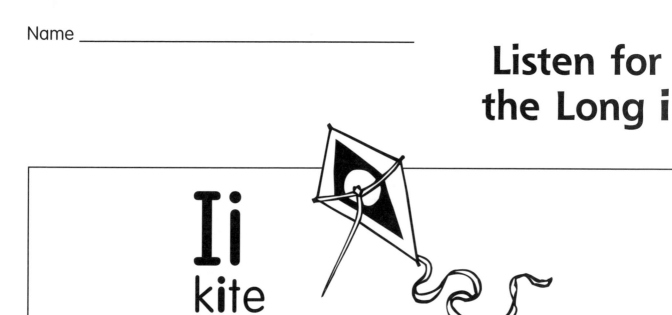

Ii
kite

Circle the pictures that have the **long i** sound.

Recognizing the sound of long i

Name _____

Pig or Kite?

Say the name of each picture.
Draw a line to the vowel sound you hear.

ĭ

pig

ī

kite

Distinguishing between the long and short sounds of **i**

Name _____

Write the vowel on the line.
Match the word to a picture.

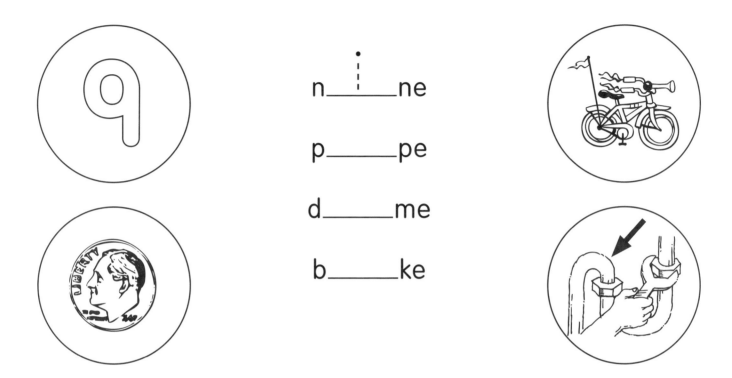

n___ne

p___pe

d___me

b___ke

___

Choose a word to write in the blank.

1. I put a _____ in my bank.

2. I can ride my _____.

3. I have _____ socks.

4. I can fix the _____.

Name _____

I Like Mike

Fill in the circle by the **long i** word that
best completes the sentence.

1. I _____ Mike.

○ **hike**   ○ **nice**   ○ **like**

2. _____ is fun.

○ **Me**   ○ **Mike**   ○ **Make**

3. Mike is _____ .

○ **dime**   ○ **bride**   ○ **nine**

4. I am _____ .

○ **Mike**   ○ **five**   ○ **dime**

5. He skates on the _____ .

○ **slide**   ○ **ice**   ○ **pipe**

6. He lets me ride his _____ .

○ **bike**   ○ **pipe**   ○ **dime**

Completing sentences with long **i** words

Listen for the Long o

O o
g**o**at

Circle the pictures that have the **long o** sound.

Recognizing the sound of long o

Name _____

Say the name of each picture.
Draw a line to the vowel sound you hear.

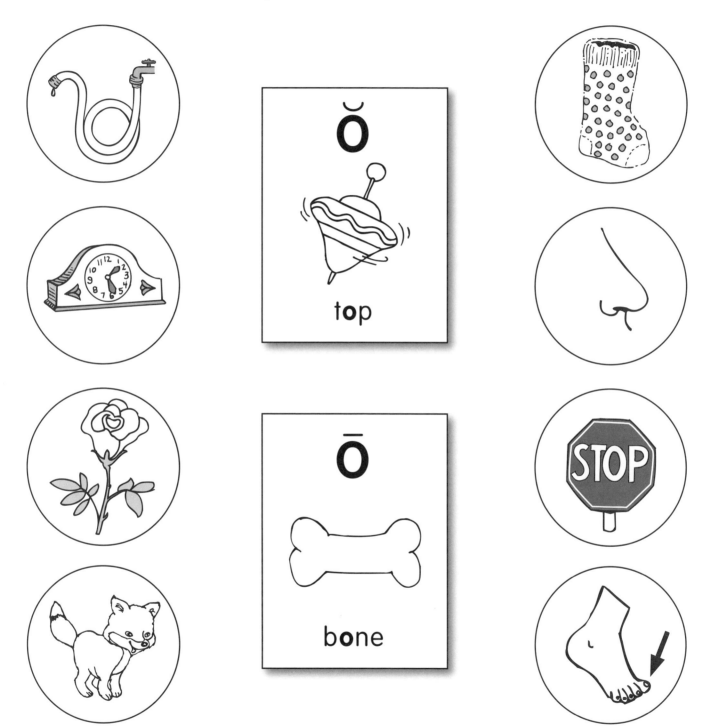

Ŏ

top

Ō

bone

Name _____

Write the vowel on the line.
Match the word to a picture.

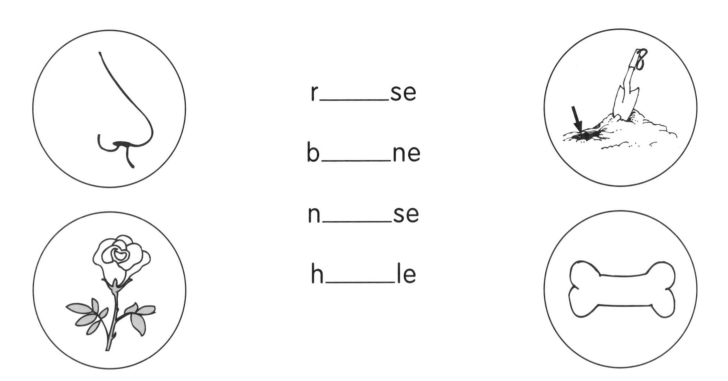

r_____se

b_____ne

n_____se

h_____le

_____

Choose a word to write in the blank.

1. The _____ is red.

2. I smell with my _____.

3. The dog ate his _____.

4. I fell in the _____ in the yard.

Name _____

Fill in the circle by the **long o** word that best completes the sentence.

---

1. Jo _____ Rose home.

   ○ **pole**   ○ **rode**   ○ **rod**

---

2. She tied the _____ to a pole.

   ○ **rope**   ○ **rip**   ○ **ripe**

---

3. Jo gave Rose a drink with the _____.

   ○ **nose**   ○ **note**   ○ **hose**

---

4. She patted Rose on the _____.

   ○ **nose**   ○ **hose**   ○ **pose**

---

5. Jo saw her dog dig a _____.

   ○ **hall**   ○ **hot**   ○ **hole**

---

6. Will he find a _____?

   ○ **stone**   ○ **bone**   ○ **box**

Completing sentences with long **o** words

Listen for the Long u

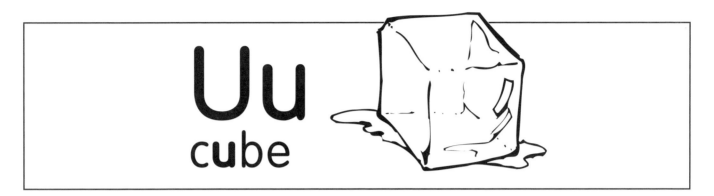

Uu
cube

Circle the pictures that have the **long u** sound.

Recognizing the sound of long u

Name _____

Cup or Cube?

Say the name of each picture.
Draw a line to the vowel sound you hear.

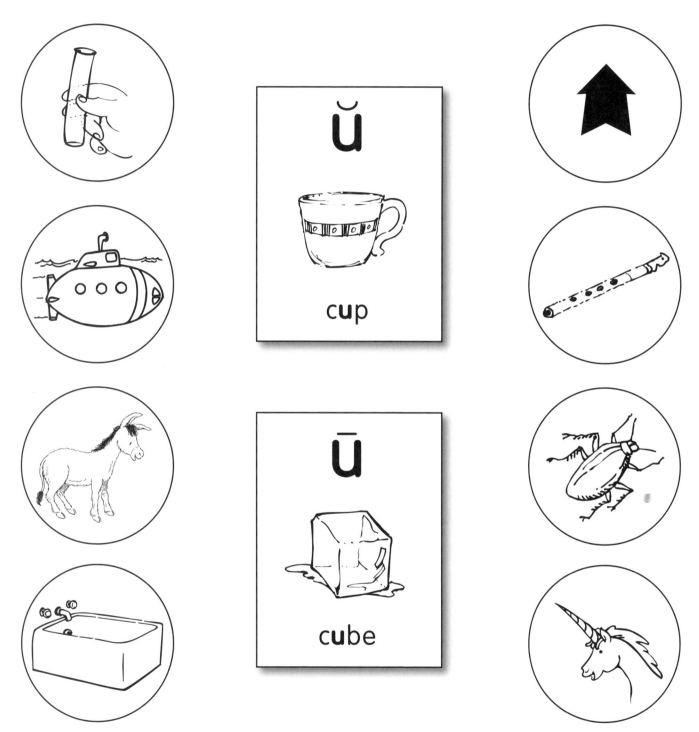

ŭ

cup

ū

cube

Distinguishing between the long and short sounds of u

Long Vowels and Short Vowels

Writing
Long u Words

Write the vowel on the line.
Match the word to a picture.

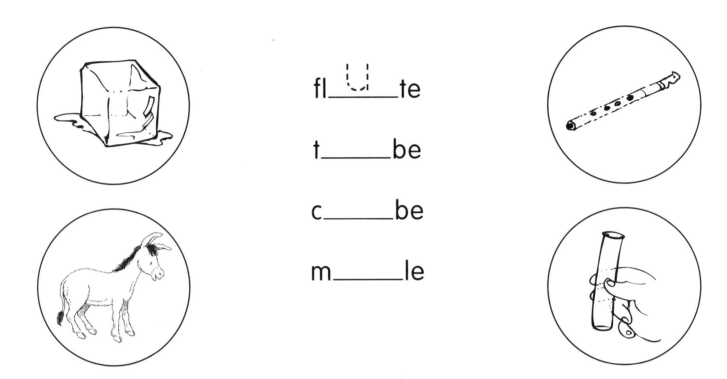

fl___te

t___be

c___be

m___le

_____

Choose a word to write in the blank.

1. Put an ice _____ in the glass.

2. I squeezed the _____ of toothpaste.

3. I play the _____.

4. The _____ ate an apple.

Name _____

Tuba Tunes

Fill in the circle by the **long u** word that
best completes the sentence.

1. Get into your _____.
  ○ **under** ○ **unit** ○ **uniforms**

2. _____, get a drum.
  ○ **Jake** ○ **June** ○ **Job**

3. Pete, get a _____.
  ○ **flat** ○ **fig** ○ **flute**

4. Sam, get a _____.
  ○ **tub** ○ **tuba** ○ **tank**

5. Play a happy _____.
  ○ **tune** ○ **tone** ○ **top**

6. We like the _____.
  ○ **make** ○ **music** ○ **mess**

*Completing sentences with long **u** words*

Name _____

Long Vowel Review

Say the name of each picture.
Fill in the circle to mark the vowel sound you hear.

ā tape

ē me

ī kite

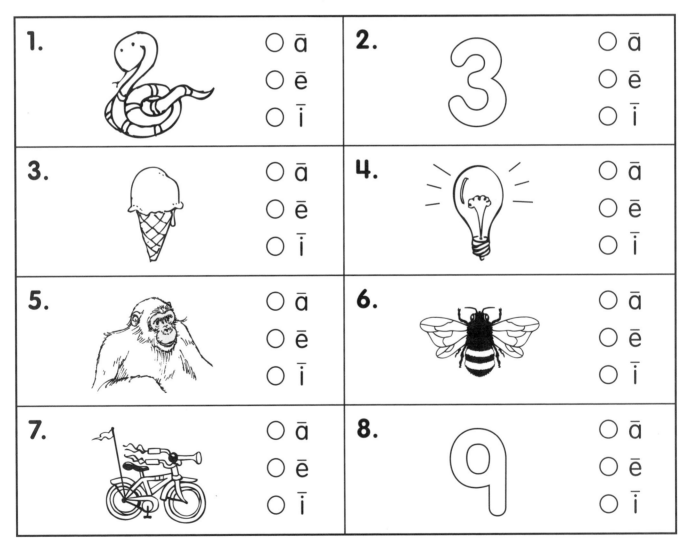

1. ○ ā ○ ē ○ ī

2. ○ ā ○ ē ○ ī

3. ○ ā ○ ē ○ ī

4. ○ ā ○ ē ○ ī

5. ○ ā ○ ē ○ ī

6. ○ ā ○ ē ○ ī

7. ○ ā ○ ē ○ ī

8. ○ ā ○ ē ○ ī

Long Vowel Review

i, o, u

| ī kite | ō boat | ū cube |

Say the name of each picture.
Fill in the circle to mark the vowel sound you hear.

1.	○ ī ○ ō ○ ū	2.	○ ī ○ ō ○ ū
3.	○ ī ○ ō ○ ū	4.	○ ī ○ ō ○ ū
5.	○ ī ○ ō ○ ū	6.	○ ī ○ ō ○ ū
7.	○ ī ○ ō ○ ū	8.	○ ī ○ ō ○ ū

Review: Long vowels i, o, u

Long Vowel Review

a, e, i, o, u

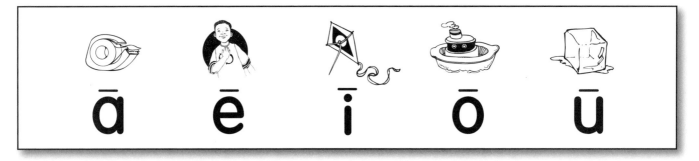

ā   ē   ī   ō   ū

Say the name of each picture.
Fill in the circle to mark the vowel sound you hear.

1.
○ ā   ○ ō
○ ē   ○ ū
○ ī

2.
○ ā   ○ ō
○ ē   ○ ū
○ ī

3.
○ ā   ○ ō
○ ē   ○ ū
○ ī

4.
○ ā   ○ ō
○ ē   ○ ū
○ ī

5.
○ ā   ○ ō
○ ē   ○ ū
○ ī

6.
○ ā   ○ ō
○ ē   ○ ū
○ ī

7.
○ ā   ○ ō
○ ē   ○ ū
○ ī

8.
○ ā   ○ ō
○ ē   ○ ū
○ ī

Review: All long vowels

Which Long Vowel?

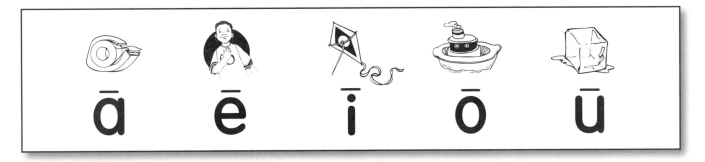

ā   ē   ī   ō   ū

Say the name of each picture.
Write the vowel sound on the line.

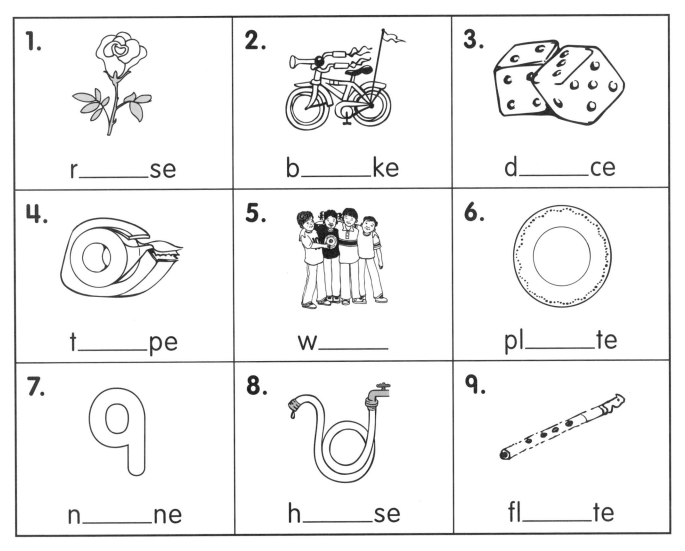

1. r____se

2. b____ke

3. d____ce

4. t____pe

5. w____

6. pl____te

7. n____ne

8. h____se

9. fl____te

Review: All long vowels

Which Long Vowel?

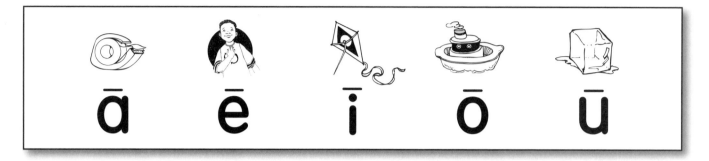

ā   ē   ī   ō   ū

Say the name of each picture.
Write the vowel sound on the line.

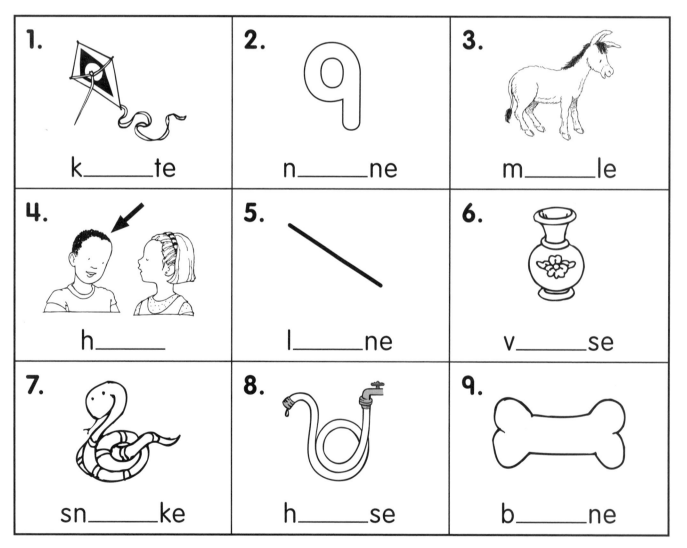

1. k____te

2. n____ne

3. m____le

4. h____

5. l____ne

6. v____se

7. sn____ke

8. h____se

9. b____ne

Review: All long vowels

Name _____

Say the name of each picture.
Write the word on the line.

1. _____	**2.** _____	**3.** _____
4. _____	**5.** _____	**6.** _____
7. _____	**8.** _____	**9.** _____

Word Box

cube	snake	smoke
tape	pine	slide
whale	pipe	nine

Review: All long vowels

©2004 by Evan-Moor Corp. • Basic Phonics Skills, Level C • EMC 3320 **Long Vowels and Short Vowels**

Name _____

Colorful Vowels

Color the parts as marked.

blue **ā**   red **ī**   green **ō**   yellow **ū**

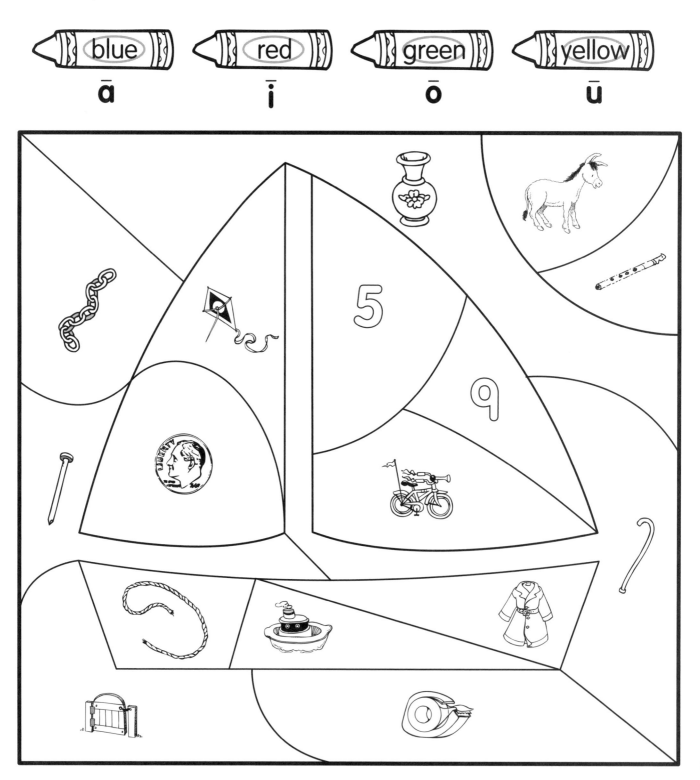

Review: All long vowels

Name _____

Read and Think

Circle the word that best completes each sentence.

1. The note was in _____.
   ○ **cape**   ○ **cod**   ○ **code**

2. His pet _____ was long.
   ○ **snake**   ○ **cap**   ○ **tape**

3. She wants an ice _____.
   ○ **cake**   ○ **cube**   ○ **cub**

4. We sat under a _____ tree.
   ○ **pine**   ○ **pole**   ○ **pin**

5. I fixed it with _____.
   ○ **tap**   ○ **tape**   ○ **time**

6. Joe _____ the bus.
   ○ **rod**   ○ **rude**   ○ **rode**

Review: All long vowels

Name _____

Silent e

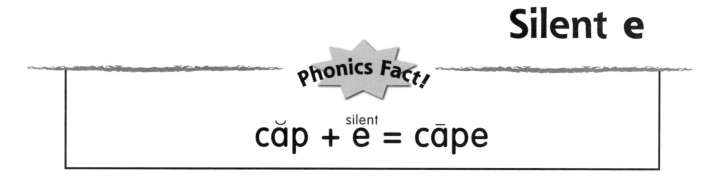
Add a silent **e**. Read the word.
Match the word to its picture.

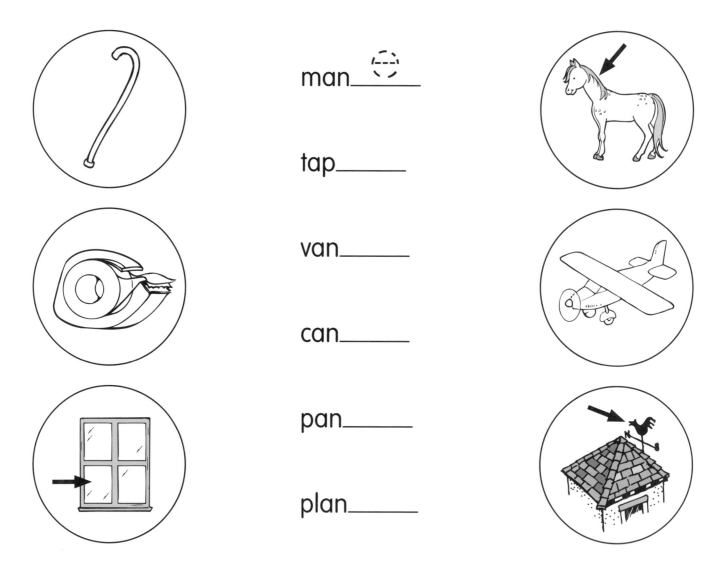

man_____

tap_____

van_____

can_____

pan_____

plan_____

Using silent e to form long vowel words

Name _____

Silent e

$$gl\breve{o}b + \overset{silent}{\bar{e}} = gl\bar{o}be$$

Add a silent **e**. Read the word.
Match the word to its picture.

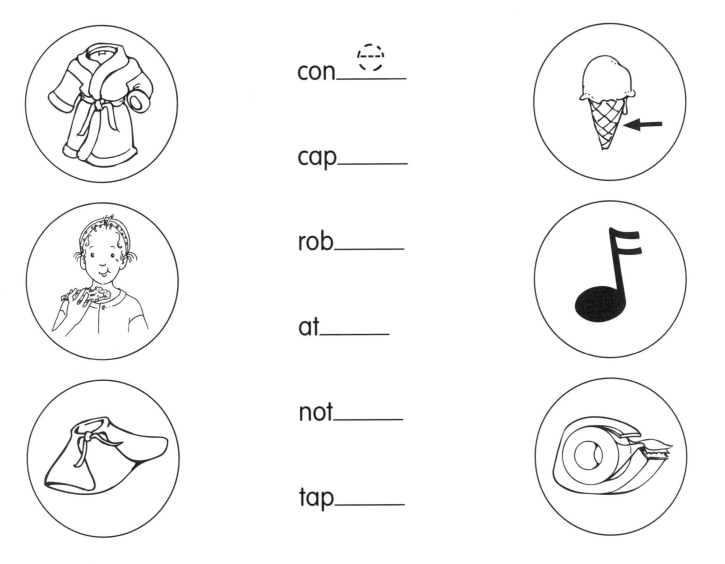

con_____

cap_____

rob_____

at_____

not_____

tap_____

Using silent **e** to form long vowel words

Name _____

Silent e

Phonics Fact!

$$b\breve{i}t + \overset{silent}{e} = b\bar{i}te$$

Add a silent **e**. Read the word.
Match the word to its picture.

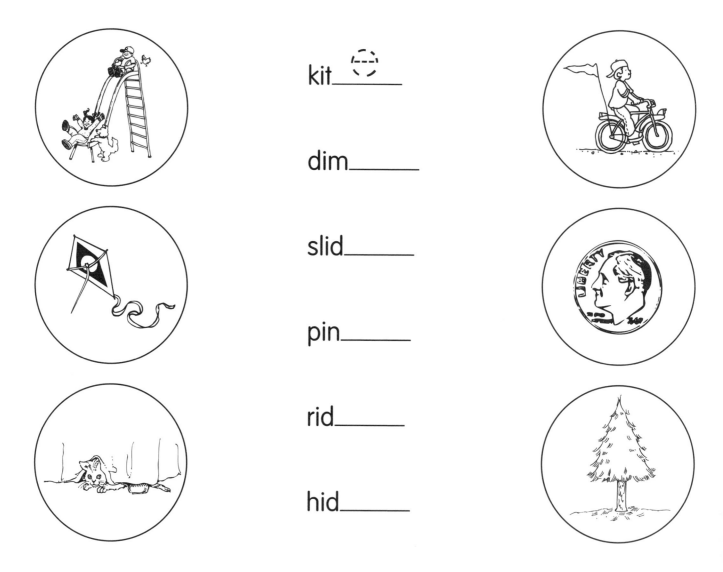

kit_____

dim_____

slid_____

pin_____

rid_____

hid_____

Using silent e to form long vowel words

Silent e

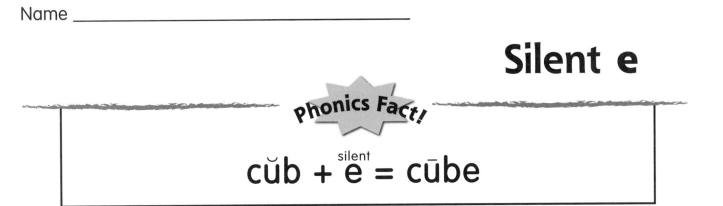

Phonics Fact!

cŭb + ^{silent} e = cūbe

Add a silent **e**. Read the word.
Match the word to its picture.

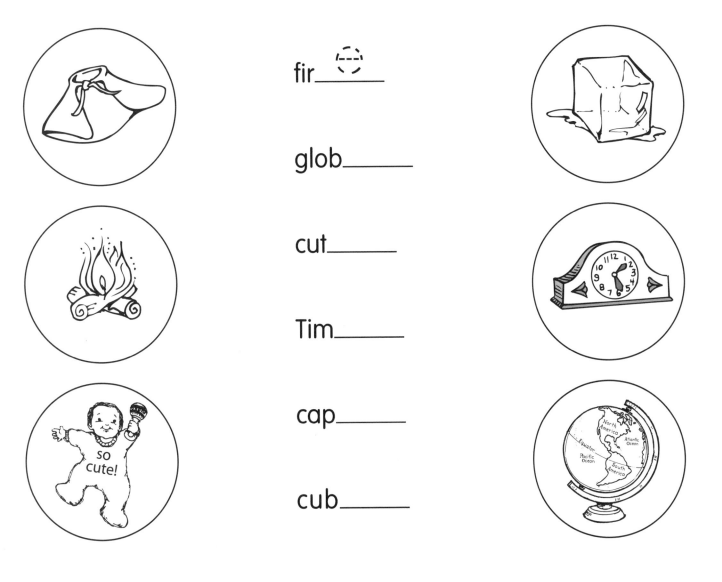

fir_____

glob_____

cut_____

Tim_____

cap_____

cub_____

Using silent e to form long vowel words

Long Vowels and Short Vowels

Name _____

It's Fun!

Circle the correct word.

1. Mike has a _____.	rob robe
2. He likes to _____ his bike.	ride rid
3. Kate has a _____ mule.	cut cute
4. The _____ is red and blue.	kite kit
5. _____ has a cake.	time Tim
6. See his _____ go.	plan plane

Reading silent e words

Name _____

A Dime

Circle the correct word.

1. Pete had a _____.	dim dime
2. He got a _____.	con cone
3. He _____ the cone.	at ate
4. _____ had a dime, too.	Kit kite
5. She got a _____.	plane plan
6. Was it a _____ plane?	hug huge

Reading silent e words

Name _____

Big Mike

Circle the correct word.

1. Mike has a brown _____.	man mane
2. He is _____.	cute cut
3. He is _____.	hug huge
4. Mike ate a big _____ of hay.	bit bite
5. He went for a _____.	ride rid
6. He liked to _____ in the barn.	hid hide

Reading silent e words

Name _____

A Cute Cub

Circle the correct word.

1. I have a toy bear _____.	cube cub
2. He is so _____.	cute cut
3. I like to _____ him.	huge hug
4. Mom loves _____ both.	use us
5. She will make a cake for _____.	us use
6. I will wash him in the _____.	tube tub

Reading silent e words

The Hard and Soft Sounds of *c, g*

BASIC **Phonics Skills**

Basic Phonics Skills, Level C • EMC 3320 • ©2004 by Evan-Moor Corp.

Name _____

Cat begins with the hard sound of the letter **c**.

cat

Circle the words that begin with the same sound as **cat**.

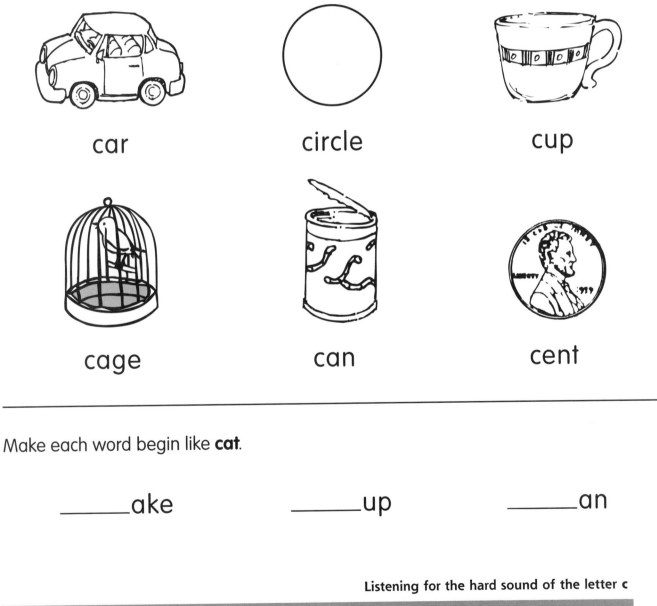

car

circle

cup

cage

can

cent

Make each word begin like **cat**.

_____ake   _____up   _____an

Listening for the hard sound of the letter **c**

The Hard and Soft
Sounds of c, g

Name _____

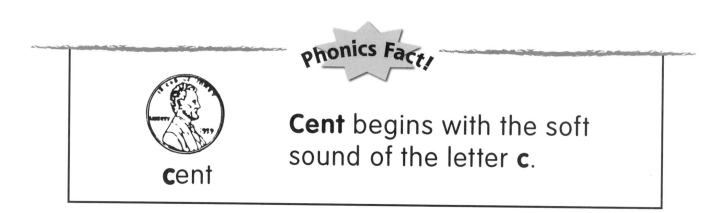

Cent begins with the soft sound of the letter **c**.

cent

Circle the words that begin with the same sound as **cent**.

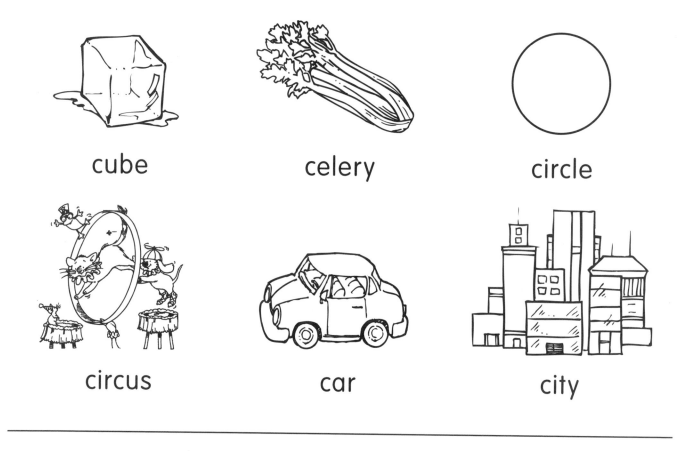

cube

celery

circle

circus

car

city

Make each word begin like **cent**.

_____ircle

_____ircus

Name _____

Make a Match

Say the name of each picture.
Listen to the sound **c** makes.
Draw a line to the correct box.

car

corn

cent

city

cape

cup

cake

cereal

candle

circle

Distinguishing between the hard and soft sounds of c

Sounds of c

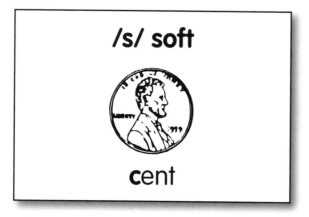

/s/ soft

cent

/k/ hard

cat

Say the name of each picture.
Mark the sound that **c** makes.

1. coat	**2. c**ow	**3. c**elery
○ /k/ ○ /s/	○ /k/ ○ /s/	○ /k/ ○ /s/
4. cape	**5. c**ity	**6. c**ake
○ /k/ ○ /s/	○ /k/ ○ /s/	○ /k/ ○ /s/

Identifying the hard and soft sounds of c

Name _____

Sounds of c

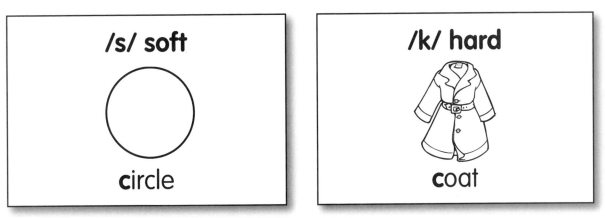

/s/ soft	/k/ hard
circle	coat

Circle the word that best completes the sentence.

1. Will Carl _____ home?	cent come
2. Cindy will _____ Mike.	call city
3. Jill needs 35 _____.	cents cold
4. Dad will drive his _____ home.	cell car
5. Will the cute _____ come?	cat circle
6. It is in its _____.	cent cage

Completing sentences with hard and soft **c** words

**The Hard and Soft
Sounds of c, g**

Name _____

Sounds of g

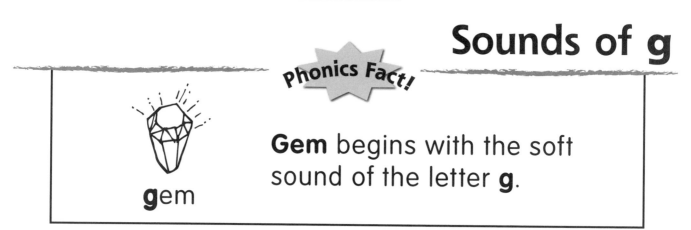

Gem begins with the soft sound of the letter **g**.

gem

Circle the words that begin with the same sound as **gem**.

giraffe

gum

general

gas

gingerbread

gold

Make each word begin like **gem**.

_____iant

_____ingerbread

Listening for the soft sound of the letter g

Name _____

Phonics Fact!

Goat begins with the hard sound of the letter **g**.

goat

Circle the words that begin with the same sound as **goat**.

gum

gem

girl

gift

gas

giant

Make each word begin like **goat**.

_____ate   _____oose

Listening for the hard sound of the letter **g**

Name _____

Make a Match

Say the name of each picture.
Listen to the sound **g** makes.
Draw a line to the correct box.

gate

general

gem

goat

gift

girl

gas

giraffe

gum

giant

Distinguishing between the hard and soft sounds of g

Name _____

Sounds of g

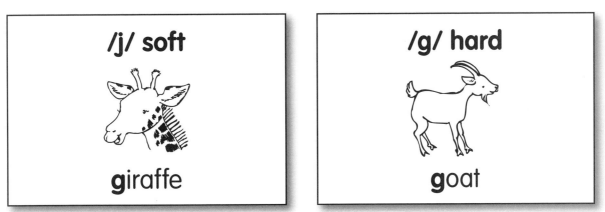

/j/ soft	/g/ hard
giraffe	goat

Say the name of each picture.
Mark the sound that **g** makes.

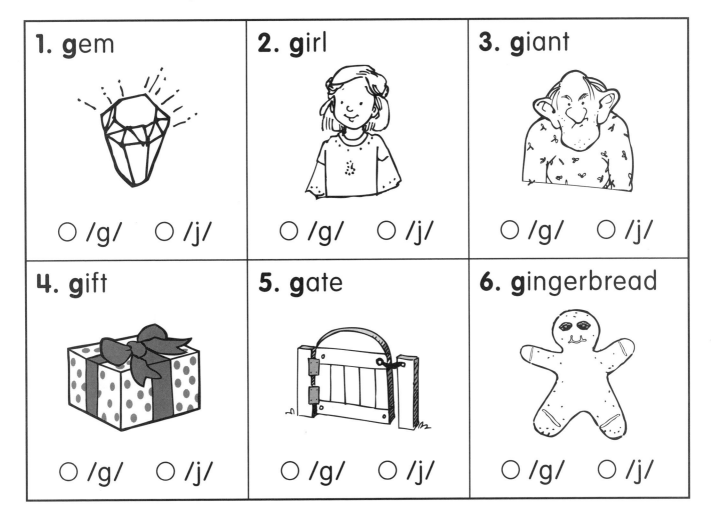

1. gem
○ /g/   ○ /j/

2. girl
○ /g/   ○ /j/

3. giant
○ /g/   ○ /j/

4. gift
○ /g/   ○ /j/

5. gate
○ /g/   ○ /j/

6. gingerbread
○ /g/   ○ /j/

Identifying the hard and soft sounds of g

Sounds of g

/j/ soft

giant

/g/ hard

gate

Circle the word that best completes the sentence.

1. Close the _____.	gate giant
2. The _____ is so tall.	giraffe gas
3. The _____ ate the gum.	gem goat
4. The car needs _____.	giant gas
5. We can play a _____.	giraffe game
6. I will give her a _____.	gem go

Completing sentences with hard and soft g words

Basic Phonics Skills, Level C • EMC 3320 • ©2004 by Evan-Moor Corp.

Review

Sounds of c, g

Read the first word in each row.
Circle the word that begins with the same sound.

1.	gate	gem	giant	garden
2.	cat	cereal	cave	cent
3.	cent	circle	cave	can
4.	coat	cab	circle	cent
5.	can	circle	come	cent
6.	giant	gas	gave	gem

Review: The hard and soft sounds of c and g

The Hard and Soft
Sounds of c, g

Beginning & Ending Consonant Digraphs

Basic Phonics Skills, Level C • EMC 3320 • ©2004 by Evan-Moor Corp.

At the Beginning

Say the name of each picture.
Listen to the beginning sound.
Draw a line to the correct box.

th

thread

sh

shoe

Distinguishing between the beginning sounds of sh and th

Name _____

Say the name of each picture.
Listen to the beginning sound.
Draw a line to the correct box.

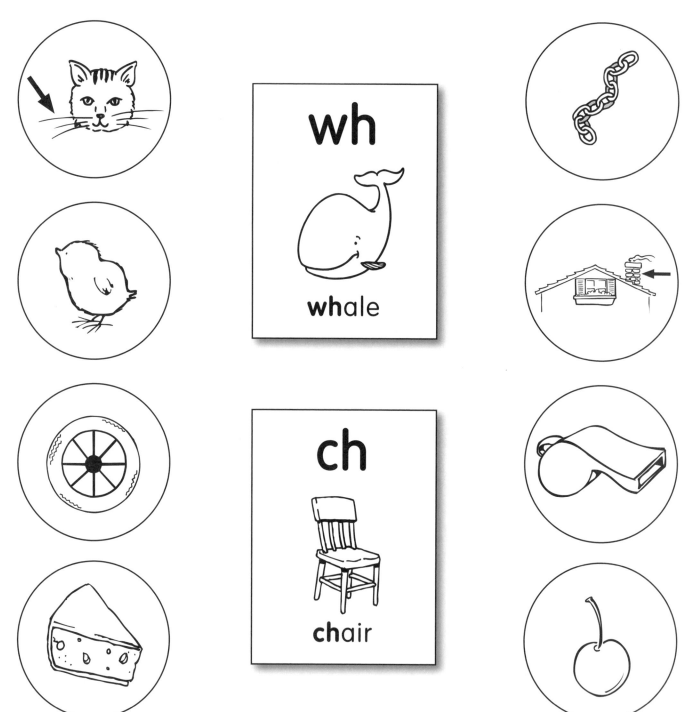

wh

whale

ch

chair

Distinguishing between the beginning sounds of **wh** and **ch**

**Beginning & Ending
Consonant Digraphs**

Basic Phonics Skills, Level C • EMC 3320 • ©2004 by Evan-Moor Corp.

Which One?

Say the name of each picture.
Fill in the circle by the beginning sound.

1.	○ ch ○ sh ○ th ○ wh	**2.**	○ ch ○ sh ○ th ○ wh
3.	○ ch ○ sh ○ th ○ wh	**4.**	○ ch ○ sh ○ th ○ wh
5.	○ ch ○ sh ○ th ○ wh	**6.**	○ ch ○ sh ○ th ○ wh
7. 30	○ ch ○ sh ○ th ○ wh	**8.**	○ ch ○ sh ○ th ○ wh

Review: Identifying the beginning digraph—sh, th, wh, ch

Match Them Up

Say the name of each picture.
Draw a line to the sound you hear at the beginning.

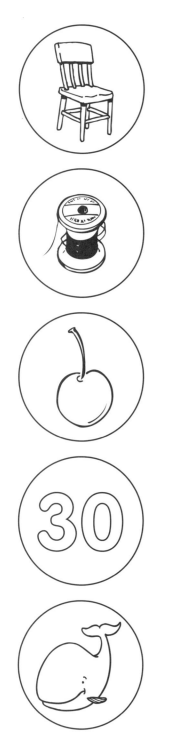

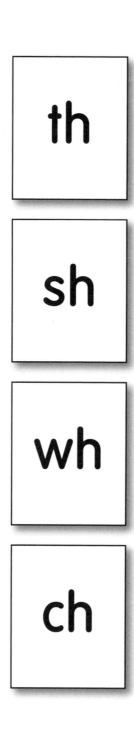

th

sh

wh

ch

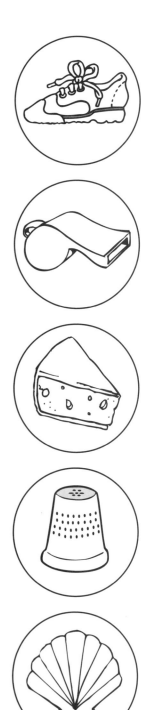

Review: Identifying consonant digraphs as beginning sounds

   Basic Phonics Skills, Level C • EMC 3320 • ©2004 by Evan-Moor Corp.

Listen and Write

sh	th	wh	ch

Fill in the missing letters.
Draw a line to the correct picture.

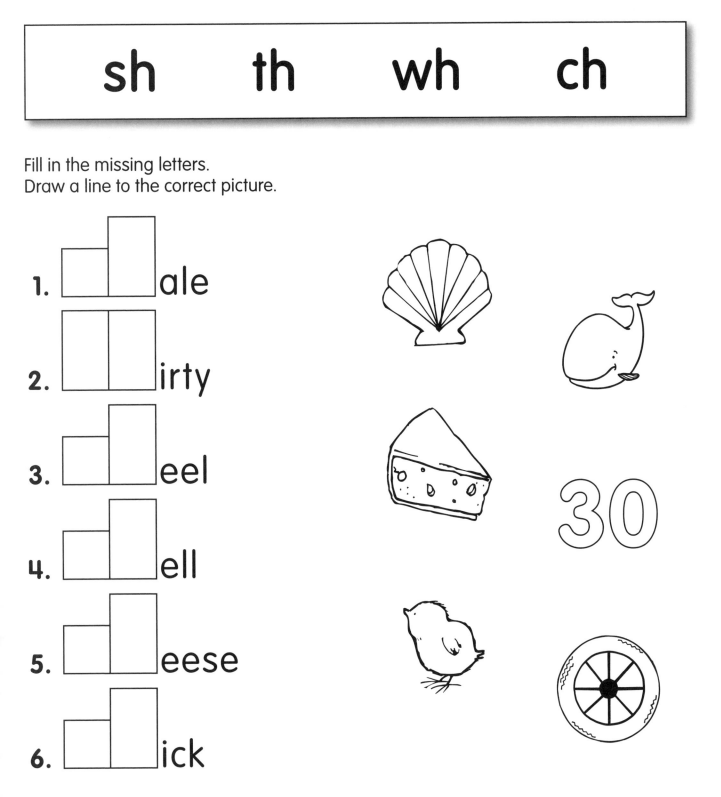

1. ☐☐ ale

2. ☐☐ irty

3. ☐☐ eel

4. ☐☐ ell

5. ☐☐ eese

6. ☐☐ ick

Review: Forming words by writing the correct beginning digraph—sh, th, wh, ch

At the End

Say the name of each picture.
Listen to the ending sound.
Draw a line to the correct box.

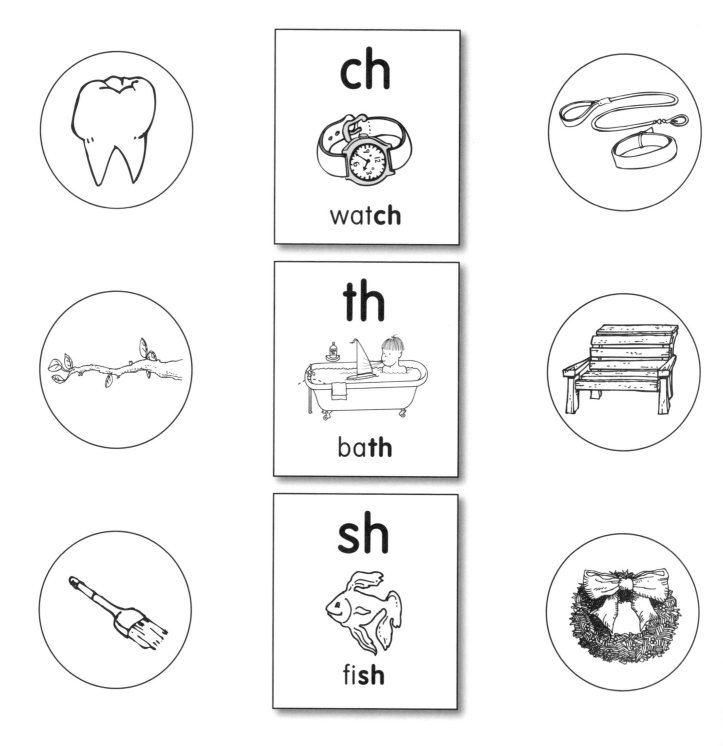

ch

watch

th

bath

sh

fish

Distinguishing among the ending sounds of ch, th, and sh

Name _____

Listen to the End

Say the name of each picture.
Fill in the circle by the sound you hear at the end.

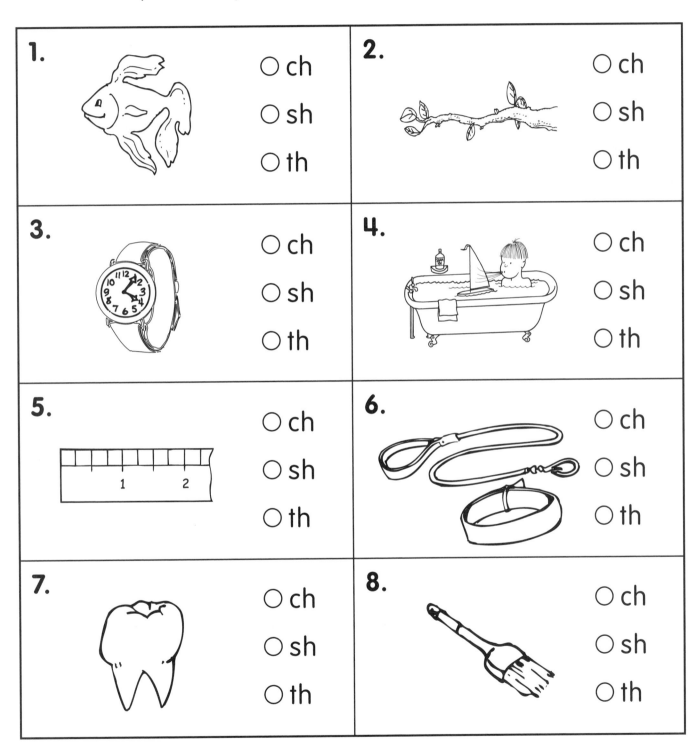

1.
○ ch
○ sh
○ th

2.
○ ch
○ sh
○ th

3.
○ ch
○ sh
○ th

4.
○ ch
○ sh
○ th

5.
○ ch
○ sh
○ th

6.
○ ch
○ sh
○ th

7.
○ ch
○ sh
○ th

8.
○ ch
○ sh
○ th

Identifying the correct ending digraph—sh, th, ch

Listen and Write

| sh | th | ch |

Fill in the missing letters.
Draw a line to the correct picture.

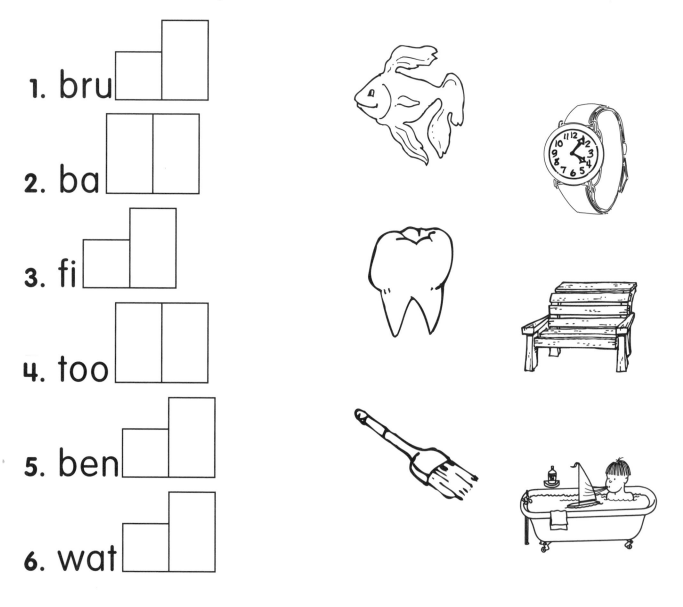

1. bru☐☐

2. ba☐☐

3. fi☐☐

4. too☐☐

5. ben☐☐

6. wat☐☐

Forming words by writing **sh, th, ch**

Beginning & Ending Consonant Digraphs

Basic Phonics Skills, Level C • EMC 3320 • ©2004 by Evan-Moor Corp.

R-Controlled Vowels

©2004 by Evan-Moor Corp. • Basic Phonics Skills, Level C • EMC 3320

Name _____

Sounds the Same

Underline **er**, **ir**, or **ur** in each word.
Draw a line to match the word to its picture.

lett**er**   b**ir**d   p**ur**se

nurse

her

fur

river

stir

shirt

Name ______________________________

Her Purple Bird

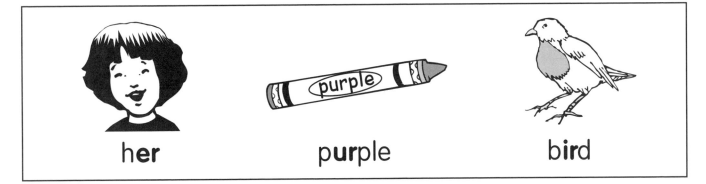

her

purple

bird

Underline the letters that make the sound of **r**.

girl	first	water	burn
finger	purse	dirt	over
curl	nurse	ladder	shirt

Write each word in the correct box.

er	**ur**	**ir**

Reading words with /er/, /ur/, /ir/

The Bird

Use the words in the box to complete the sentences.

1. The _____bird_____ sat in her nest.

2. The nest was in the _____ tree.

3. The bird was _____ and black.

4. The tree was by a _____.

5. A rock was in the _____.

6. A _____ sat on the rock.

7. The bird flew _____ the turtle.

8. Will she _____ back to her nest?

Word Box		
water	over	river
bird	fir	turtle
turn	purple	

Name _____

Make a Match

Say the name of each picture.
Listen for **ar** or **or**.
Draw a line to match each picture to the correct box.

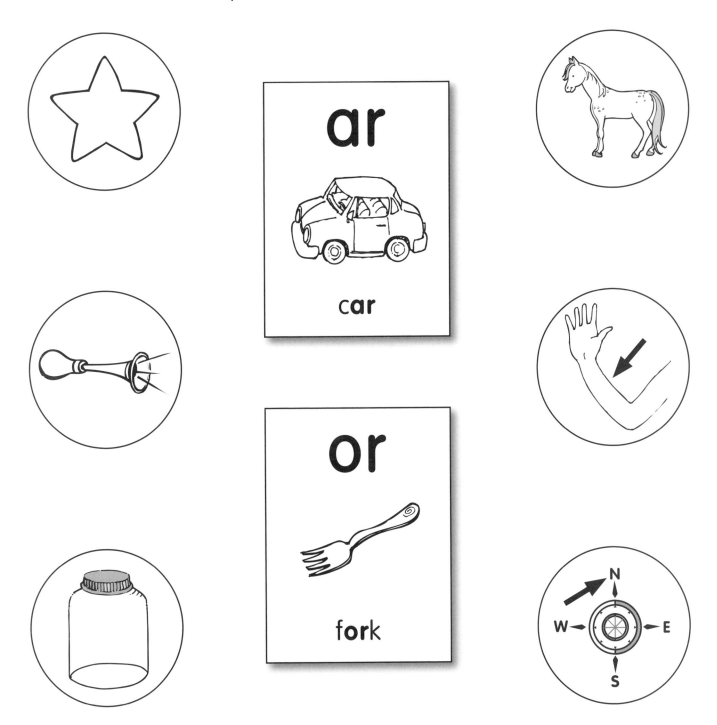

ar
car

or
fork

Name _____

What Do You Hear?

The h<u>or</u>se is
in the b<u>ar</u>n.

Say the name of each picture.
Fill in the circle by the sound you hear.

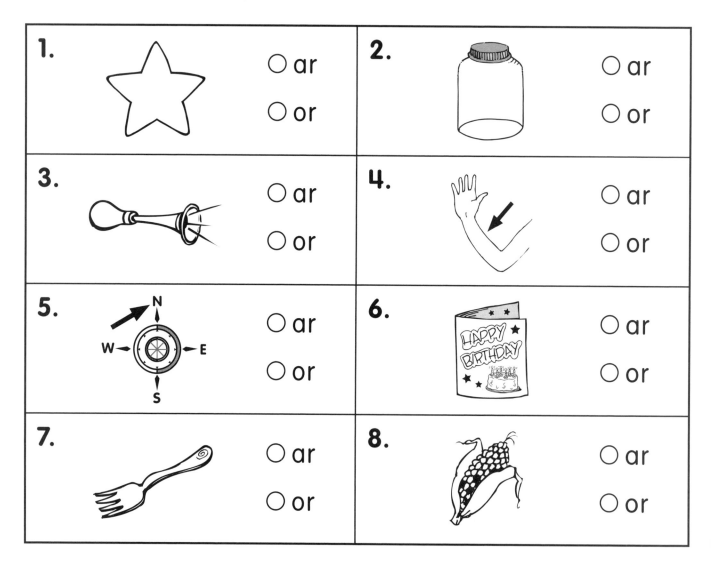

1.　　○ ar　　○ or

2.　　○ ar　　○ or

3.　　○ ar　　○ or

4.　　○ ar　　○ or

5.　　○ ar　　○ or

6.　　○ ar　　○ or

7.　　○ ar　　○ or

8.　　○ ar　　○ or

Distinguishing between the sounds of or and ar in words

Name _____

What's Missing?

Write the missing letters on the lines.

ar	or

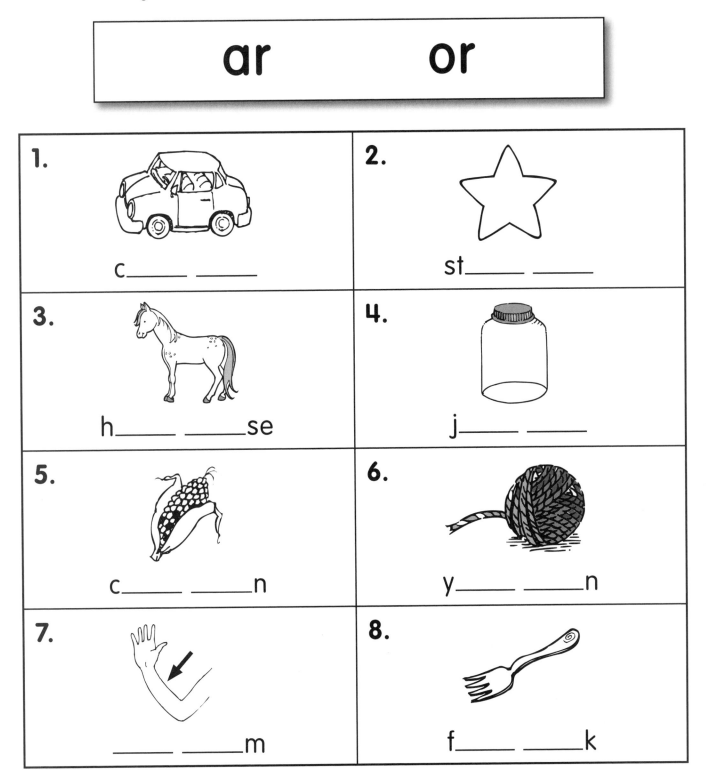

1. c_____ _____

2. st_____ _____

3. h_____ _____se

4. j_____ _____

5. c_____ _____n

6. y_____ _____n

7. _____ _____m

8. f_____ _____k

Name _____

Name each picture.
Fill in the circle to show which sound you hear.

1. ○ ar ○ or ○ ir

2. ○ ar ○ or ○ ur

3. ○ ar ○ ir ○ ur

4. ○ ar ○ or ○ ir

5. ○ er ○ or ○ ur

6. ○ ar ○ or ○ ur

7. ○ ar ○ or ○ ir

8. ○ er ○ or ○ ur

9. ○ ar ○ ir ○ ur

Review: Identifying the correct r-controlled vowels

Basic Phonics Skills, Level C • EMC 3320 • ©2004 by Evan-Moor Corp.

Name _____

The Ride

Circle the correct word.
Write the word on the line.

1. The _____ wanted to go for a ride.	park girl
2. She went to the _____.	born barn
3. The _____ was in his stall.	horse heard
4. She put her _____ over him.	arm jar
5. She jumped on and rode _____.	born north
6. She rode over the _____.	ladder river

Review: Completing sentences with r-controlled vowels

R-Controlled Vowels

Review

Write the correct word on the line.

1. It was a _____ day.

2. A _____ skipped
down the street.

3. She went to mail a _____.

4. Her _____ were cold.

5. She put on her _____.

6. Now she felt _____.

7. Then she went to the _____.

8. She played until it was _____.

Word Box			
dark	winter	warm	park
arms	sweater	girl	letter

Review: Completing sentences with r-controlled vowels

Basic Phonics Skills, Level C • EMC 3320 • ©2004 by Evan-Moor Corp.

Long Vowel Digraphs, *oo* Digraphs, and Long Vowel Sounds of *y*

BASIC Phonics Skills

New Spellings for Long a

Say the name of each picture. Fill in the missing letters that make the **long a** sound.

rain   **tray**

1. tr_____ _____n

2. ch_____ _____n

3. sn_____ _____l

4. h_____ _____

5. p_____ _____l

6. j_____ _____

Word Box

jay	train	snail
chain	pail	hay

Recognizing long **a** spelling patterns

Name _____

Pick the parts that spell the name of the object.
Write them together on the line.

t	tr	sn
h	p	n

-ay
-ail

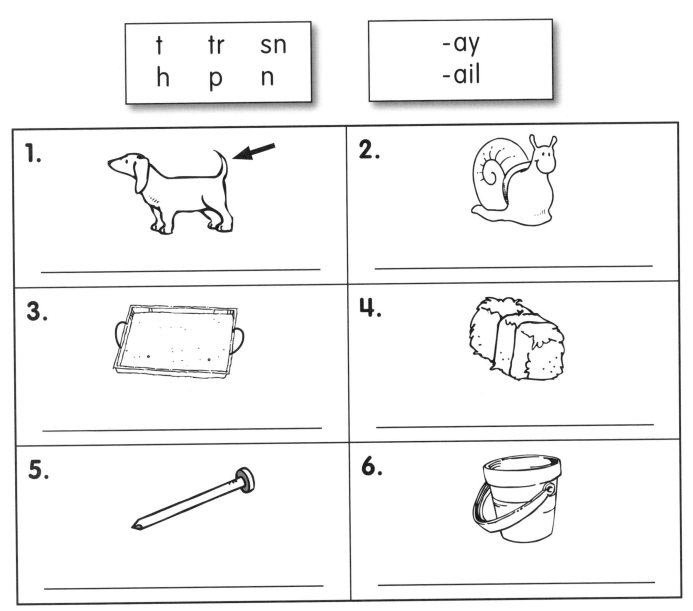

1. _____

2. _____

3. _____

4. _____

5. _____

6. _____

Circle the letters that make the **long a** sound.

rail   tray   say

lay   sail   hail

Writing words with ai, ay

Name _____

Listening for Long a

Make new words. Write a letter or letters on each line.

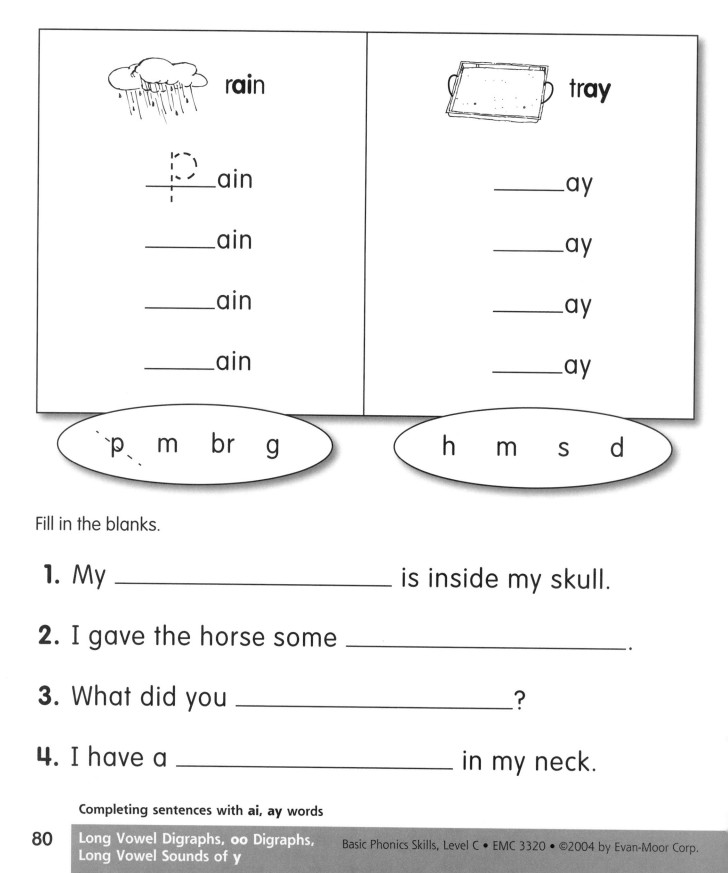

rain

_____ p ain

_____ ain

_____ ain

_____ ain

p   m   br   g

tray

_____ ay

_____ ay

_____ ay

_____ ay

h   m   s   d

Fill in the blanks.

1. My _____ is inside my skull.

2. I gave the horse some _____.

3. What did you _____?

4. I have a _____ in my neck.

Completing sentences with ai, ay words

 Long Vowel Digraphs, oo Digraphs, Long Vowel Sounds of y   Basic Phonics Skills, Level C • EMC 3320 • ©2004 by Evan-Moor Corp.

Name _____

Fill in the circle by the word that best completes the sentence.

1. The _____ is in its nest.
   - ● **jay**   ○ **day**   ○ **hay**

2. A _____ goes on tracks.
   - ○ **stain**   ○ **train**   ○ **brain**

3. Jake likes to _____ games.
   - ○ **way**   ○ **say**   ○ **play**

4. The _____ on my bike broke.
   - ○ **rain**   ○ **chain**   ○ **gain**

5. I like to _____.
   - ○ **sail**   ○ **hail**   ○ **fail**

6. He made a vase with _____.
   - ○ **tray**   ○ **stay**   ○ **clay**

Completing sentences with **ai**, **ay** words

Name _____

Ray and Jay

Fill in the missing words.

1. Ray and _____ will

_____ the fence.

2. Dad will _____ them to do
the job.

3. Dad gave them _____ paint.

4. They put the paint in a _____.

5. Dad said they will _____ ball when they
are done.

Word Box		
pail	paint	pay
Jay	play	gray

Completing sentences with **ai**, **ay** words

Long Vowel Digraphs, oo Digraphs,
Long Vowel Sounds of y Basic Phonics Skills, Level C • EMC 3320 • ©2004 by Evan-Moor Corp.

Name _____

Say the name of each picture.
Fill in the missing letters that make the **long e** sound.

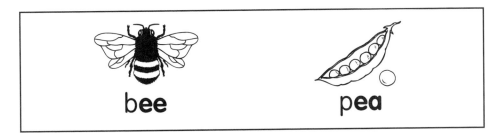

b**ee**　　　　p**ea**

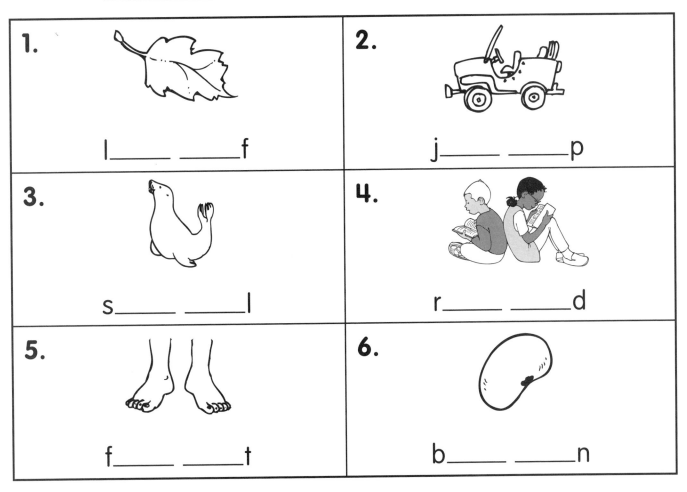

1. l_____ _____f

2. j_____ _____p

3. s_____ _____l

4. r_____ _____d

5. f_____ _____t

6. b_____ _____n

Word Box

bean	leaf	jeep
read	seal	feet

Recognizing long e spelling patterns

Match Them Up

Pick the parts that spell the name of the object.
Write them together on the line.

b	f
p	s
ch	p

-eet
-ea
-eek

1.

_____

2.

_____

3.

_____

4.

_____

5.

_____

6.

_____

Circle the letters that make the **long e** sound.

meet	tea	week
team	flea	mean

Writing words with **ea, ee**

Name _____

Which e?

Phonics Fact!

Long e sounds

e   ee   ea

Say the name of each picture.
Write the words on the lines.

1.

2.

3.

4.

5.

6.

Word Box

she	we	beet	feet
sea	bean	pea	me

Writing words with ee, ea

Name _____

Make new words. Write a letter on each line.

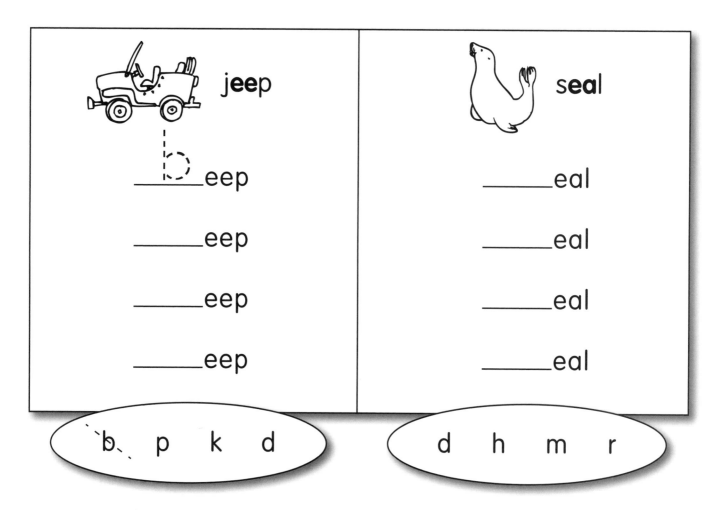

jeep

_____eep

_____eep

_____eep

_____eep

s**ea**l

_____eal

_____eal

_____eal

_____eal

b   p   k   d

d   h   m   r

Circle the word that best completes the sentence.

1. Get into the _____ .

       jeep   **beep**

2. The _____ is in the water.

      deal   **seal**

Completing sentences with ee, ea words

Long Vowel Digraphs, oo Digraphs, Long Vowel Sounds of y   Basic Phonics Skills, Level C • EMC 3320 • ©2004 by Evan-Moor Corp.

Name _____

Fill in the circle by the word that best completes the sentence.

1. The _____ drove away.
   ○ **jeep**   ○ **peep**   ○ **beep**

2. Green _____ are good to eat.
   ○ **tea**   ○ **beans**   ○ **fleas**

3. I have two _____.
   ○ **beet**   ○ **meet**   ○ **feet**

4. I will plant the _____.
   ○ **deed**   ○ **seed**   ○ **need**

5. The _____ can buzz.
   ○ **bee**   ○ **he**   ○ **me**

6. The _____ is in the water.
   ○ **deal**   ○ **real**   ○ **seal**

Completing sentences with **ee, ea** words

Drum Beat

Fill in the missing words.

1. Ben _____ on his drum.

2. "This is a _____ drum," he said.

3. His sister yelled, "_____ stop!

I can't _____!"

4. Ben stopped and got in his _____.

5. He drove down the _____.

6. His sister went to sleep. She had a good

_____.

Word Box			
flea	sleep	beat	Please
street	neat	dream	jeep

Name _____

Say the name of each picture.
Fill in the missing letters that make the **long i** sound.

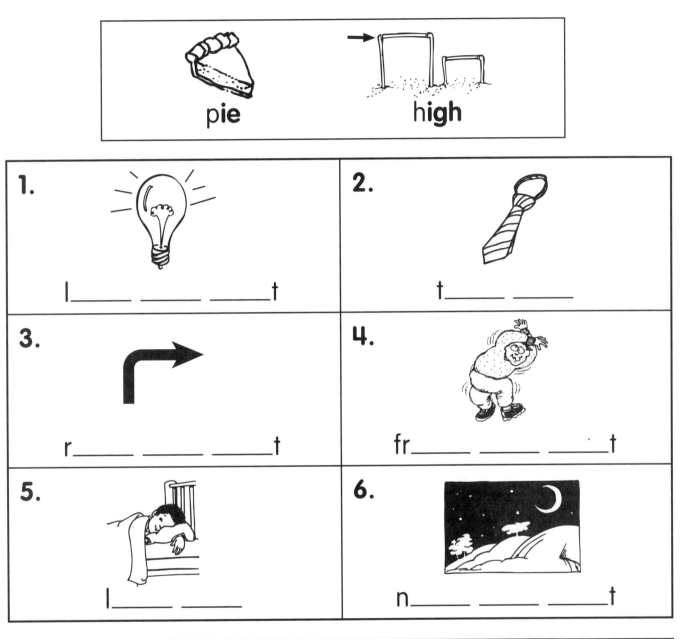

p**ie**   h**igh**

1. l_____ _____t

2. t_____ _____

3. r_____ _____ ____t

4. fr_____ _____ ____t

5. l_____ _____

6. n_____ _____ _____t

Word Box

right	lie	light
tie	fright	night

Recognizing long i spelling patterns

Match Them Up

Pick a word part from each box.
Write them together on the line.

| p n kn |
| t l r |

| -ie |
| -ight |

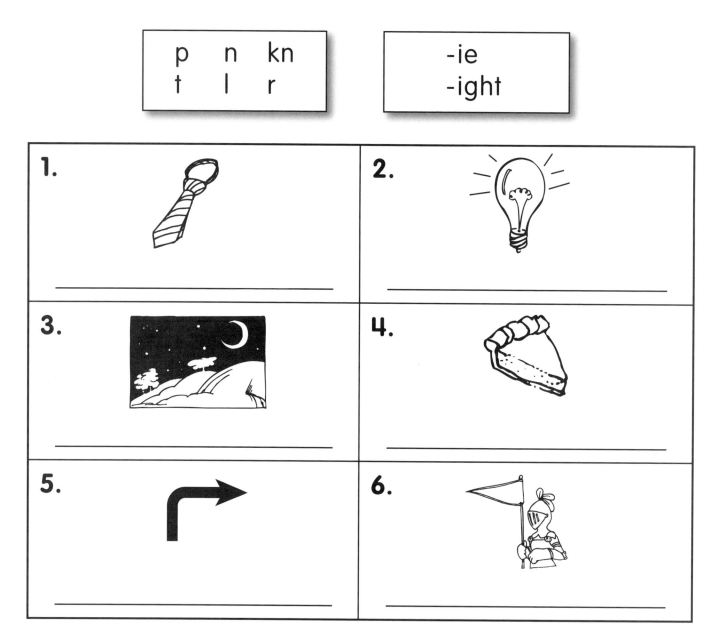

1.

2.

_____

_____

3.

4.

_____

_____

5.

6.

_____

_____

Circle the letters that make the **long i** sound.

lie   sight   might

bright   fight   die

Writing words with ie, igh

Name _____

Which i?

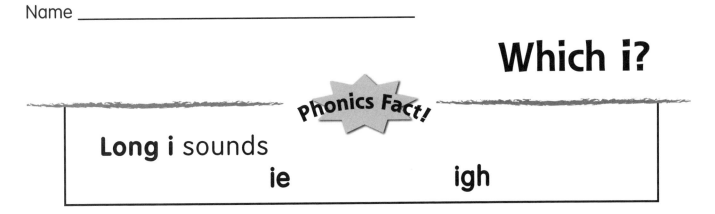

Phonics Fact!

Long i sounds

ie   igh

Write the word on the line that names the picture.
Then circle the letters that make the **long i** sound.

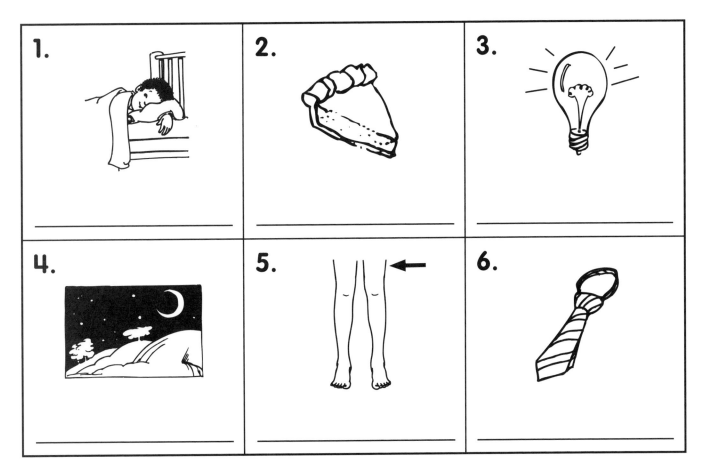

Word Box

tie	thigh	light	right
sight	pie	night	lie

Long Vowel Digraphs, **oo** Digraphs,
Long Vowel Sounds of **y**

91

Name _____

Make new words. Write a letter on each line.

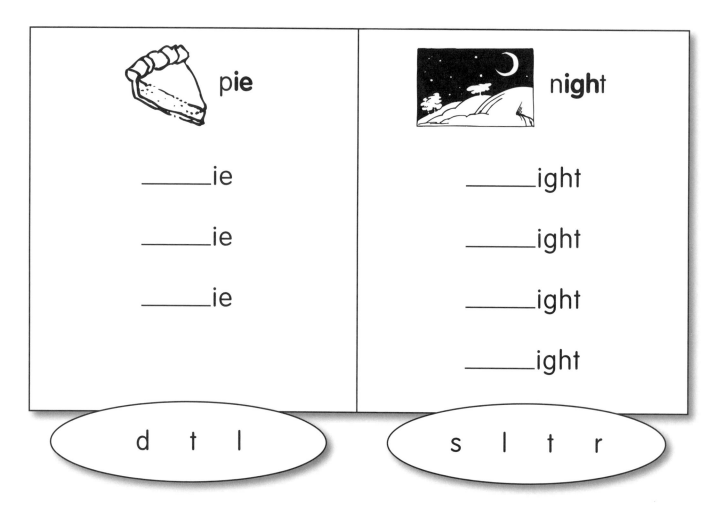

p**ie**

_____ie

_____ie

_____ie

d   t   l

n**igh**t

_____ight

_____ight

_____ight

_____ight

s   l   t   r

Circle the word that best completes the sentence.

1. Turn _____ at the corner.

right   **fight**

2. I like apple _____.

tie   **pie**

3. My shoes are too _____.

tight   **sight**

Completing sentences with **ie**, **igh** words

Name _____

Reading Words with Long i

Fill in the circle by the word that best completes the sentence.

---

1. Day is not the same as _____.

　○ **light**　　　○ **fight**　　　○ **night**

---

2. It is _____ to lie down.

　○ **time**　　　○ **dime**　　　○ **lime**

---

3. The _____ tree is so big.

　○ **fine**　　　○ **line**　　　○ **pine**

---

4. The _____ is off.

　○ **sight**　　　○ **light**　　　○ **tight**

---

5. May I eat the _____?

　○ **pie**　　　○ **tie**　　　○ **lie**

---

6. He will put on his _____.

　○ **pie**　　　○ **tie**　　　○ **lie**

Completing sentences with ie, igh words

Name _____

A Fine Night

Fill in the missing words.

1. It is a fine _____. ☆

2. The moon is _____
over the trees.

3. It gives a bright _____.

4. It is such a pretty _____!

Word Box		
might	high	light
night	sight	tight

Completing sentences with ie, igh words

Name _____

Say the name of each picture.
Fill in the missing letters that make the **long o** sound.

boa**t**	sn**ow**	t**oe**

1. b____ ____

2. c____ ____t

3. h____ ____

4. cr____ ____

5. t____ ____d

6. g____ ____t

Word Box

mow	goat	doe	hoe
coat	bow	toad	crow

Recognizing long o spelling patterns

Match Them Up

Pick the parts that spell the name of the object.
Write them together on the line.

t	m
sn	h
b	g

-ow
-oat
-oe

1. _____

2. _____

3. _____

4. _____

5. _____

6. _____

Circle the letters that make the **long o** sound.

doe   Joe   moat

float   know   low

Writing words with **oa, oe, ow**

Name _____

Which o?

Long o sounds

oe   **oa**   **ow**

Write the word on the line.
Circle the letters that make the **long o** sound.

1.

2.

3.

4.

5.

6.

Word Box

| boat | doe | blow | snow |
| Joe | toad | crow | goat |

Writing words with oa, oe, ow

Listen for Long o

Make new words. Write a letter on each line.

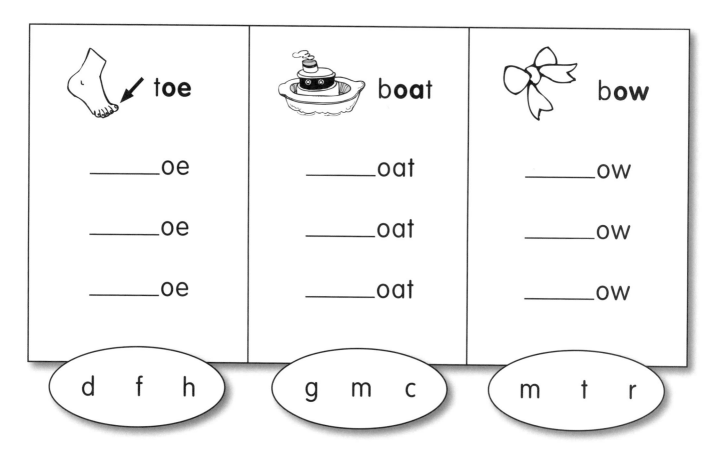

toe

_____oe

_____oe

_____oe

d   f   h

boat

_____oat

_____oat

_____oat

g   m   c

bow

_____ow

_____ow

_____ow

m   t   r

Circle the word that best completes the sentence.

1. Dig the dirt with a _____. **bone   hoe**

2. Get into the _____. **boat   oat**

3. Tie it in a _____. **tow   bow**

Name _____

Fill in the circle by the word that best completes the sentence.

1. Joe has a pet _____.
   ○ **goat**　　　○ **coat**　　　○ **boat**

2. The _____ jumped away.
   ○ **road**　　　○ **toad**　　　○ **load**

3. See the _____ fall.
   ○ **low**　　　○ **bow**　　　○ **snow**

4. I hit my _____.
   ○ **Joe**　　　○ **toe**　　　○ **hoe**

5. My dad is the _____ of our team.
   ○ **foam**　　　○ **soak**　　　○ **coach**

6. I like your red _____.
   ○ **mow**　　　○ **bow**　　　○ **low**

Completing sentences with oa, oe, ow words

Name _____

Stuck in the Snow

Fill in the missing words.

1. _____ put on his

   winter _____.

2. He put a _____ of bricks
   in his truck.

3. Away he went down the _____.

4. It started to _____.

5. After a while, the truck did not go. Then a

   _____ truck came along. Lucky Joe!

Word Box				
snow	road	boat	Joe	load
bow	tow	coat	toad	goat

Completing sentences with **oa, oe, ow** words

Name _____

Spellings for **oo**

Say the name of each picture.
Fill in the missing letter or letters that make
the **long u** sound.

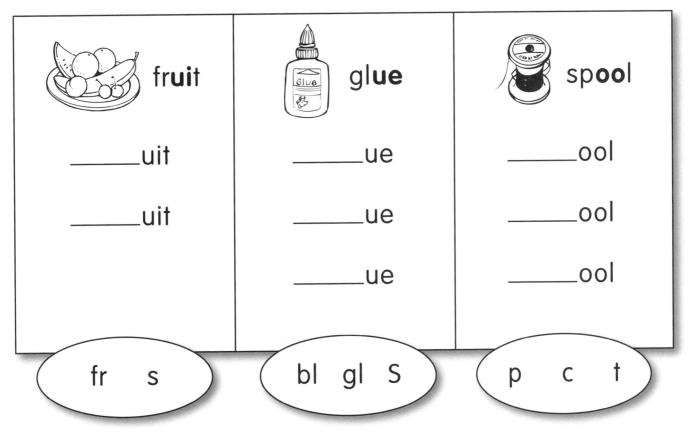

fr**ui**t	gl**ue**	sp**oo**l
_____uit	_____ue	_____ool
_____uit	_____ue	_____ool
	_____ue	_____ool

fr s	bl gl S	p c t

Color the picture. Read the sentence.
Circle the letters that make the **long u** sound.

blue suit

cutting tool

glue

Sue is at school.

Recognizing oo spelling patterns

Name _____

Draw lines to match the words and pictures.

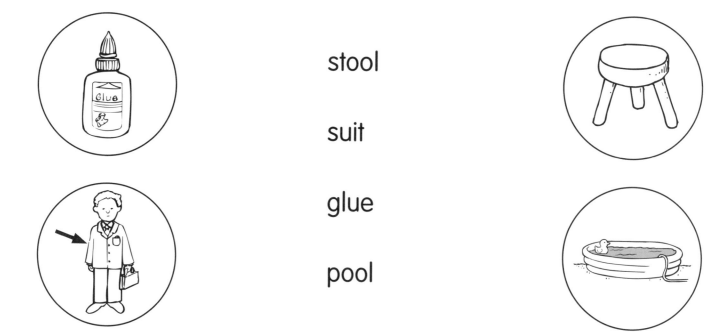

stool

suit

glue

pool

Circle the word that best completes the sentence.

1. You can fix it with _____.   **glue   blue**

2. His _____ is too big.   **juice   suit**

3. Please sit on the _____.   **stool   pool**

4. I can swim in the _____.   **tool   pool**

Writing words with ue, ui, oo

Name _____

Pick the parts that spell the name of the object.
Write them together on the line.

| gl   sch |
| fr   p |

| -uit |
| -ue |
| -ool |

1.

_____

2.

_____

3.

_____

4.

_____

Circle the letters that make the **oo** sound.

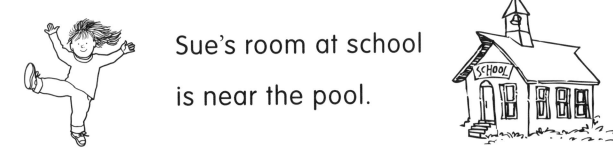

Sue's room at school

is near the pool.

Writing words with ue, ui, oo

Name _____

Which oo?

Write the word on the line.
Circle the letters that make the sound of **oo**.

1.	**2.**	**3.**

Word Box

juice   glue   goose

Circle the letters that make the sound of **oo**.

Sit on the blue stool and

drink the cool juice.

Writing words with ue, ui, oo

Name _____

Read **oo** Words

Fill in the circle by the word that best completes the sentence.

1. Luke has a new blue _____.
○ **fruit**   ○ **suit**

2. The sky is a bright _____.
○ **blue**   ○ **cue**

3. I like orange _____.
○ **suit**   ○ **juice**

4. Look at the race car _____ away.
○ **zoom**   ○ **boom**

5. It's raining. Put on your _____.
○ **toots**   ○ **boots**

6. That library book is _____ today.
○ **due**   ○ **glue**

Completing sentences with ue, ui, oo words

Name _____

A Moose on the Loose

Fill in the missing words.

1. "A _____ is _____!"

   yelled _____keeper Ruth.

2. "I'll put a _____ of _____

   in a box," said zookeeper _____.

3. "The moose will want to eat _____.

4. Then we can _____ a rope over him."

Word Box

zoo	loop	Sue	scoop
food	loose	soon	moose

Completing sentences with ue, ui, oo words

Name _____

Sounds of Yy

When **y** is at the end of a word, it has the **long i** sound or the **long e** sound.

Say the name of each picture.
Draw a line to the correct ending sound.

cry

fly

y = $\bar{i}$

bunny

happy

sunny

y = $\bar{e}$

fry

lady

why

Distinguishing between the long i and long e sounds of y

Name _____

Listen to y

Say the name of each picture.
Fill in the circle by the sound that **y** makes.

1. fly   ◯ ī   ◯ ē

2. bunny   ◯ ī   ◯ ē

3. sunny   ◯ ī   ◯ ē

4. cry   ◯ ī   ◯ ē

5. happy   ◯ ī   ◯ ē

6. lady   ◯ ī   ◯ ē

7. fry   ◯ ī   ◯ ē

8. cherry   ◯ ī   ◯ ē

Distinguishing between the long i and long e sounds of y

Basic Phonics Skills, Level C • EMC 3320 • ©2004 by Evan-Moor Corp.

What's the Rule?

Read each word.
Fill in the circle by the sound that **y** makes.
Then fill in the circle to tell how many syllables there are.

1. why	○ ī ○ ē	○ 1 ○ 2	**2.** fry	○ ī ○ ē	○ 1 ○ 2
3. funny	○ ī ○ ē	○ 1 ○ 2	**4.** sky	○ ī ○ ē	○ 1 ○ 2
5. lady	○ ī ○ ē	○ 1 ○ 2	**6.** baby	○ ī ○ ē	○ 1 ○ 2
7. try	○ ī ○ ē	○ 1 ○ 2	**8.** party	○ ī ○ ē	○ 1 ○ 2

Finish the rule.

Rule 1

At the end of a 1-syllable word, **y** has the long _____ sound.

Rule 2

At the end of a 2-syllable word, **y** has the long _____ sound.

Distinguishing between the long i and long e sounds of y

Name _____

The Baby

Pick the word that best completes each sentence.

1. The _____ is cute.

2. Will she _____?

3. She looks up at the _____.

4. _____ is baby sad?

5. Give her the little _____.

6. Now she is _____.

Word Box		
Why	bunny	sky
baby	cry	happy

Completing sentences with "y" words

Long Vowel Digraphs, **oo** Digraphs, Long Vowel Sounds of **y**   Basic Phonics Skills, Level C • EMC 3320 • ©2004 by Evan-Moor Corp.

Name _____

Make It Rhyme

Fill in the circle by the word that best completes the rhyme.

1. I have a bunny named _____.
  ○ **Sunny**   ○ **pony**

2. Sunny is _____.
  ○ **pony**   ○ **funny**

3. That's Tony. He's my _____.
  ○ **penny**   ○ **pony**

4. Denny has a new _____.
  ○ **penny**   ○ **party**

5. Sad songs make me cry. I don't know _____.
  ○ **sky**   ○ **why**

6. The lark will fly high in the _____.
  ○ **sky**   ○ **sly**

Completing sentences with "y" words

Name _____

Spell It!

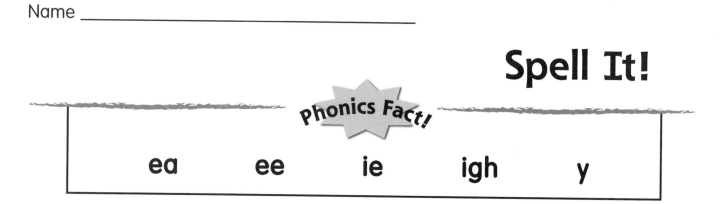

| ea | ee | ie | igh | y |

Say the name of each picture.
Choose the correct spelling for the missing letters.

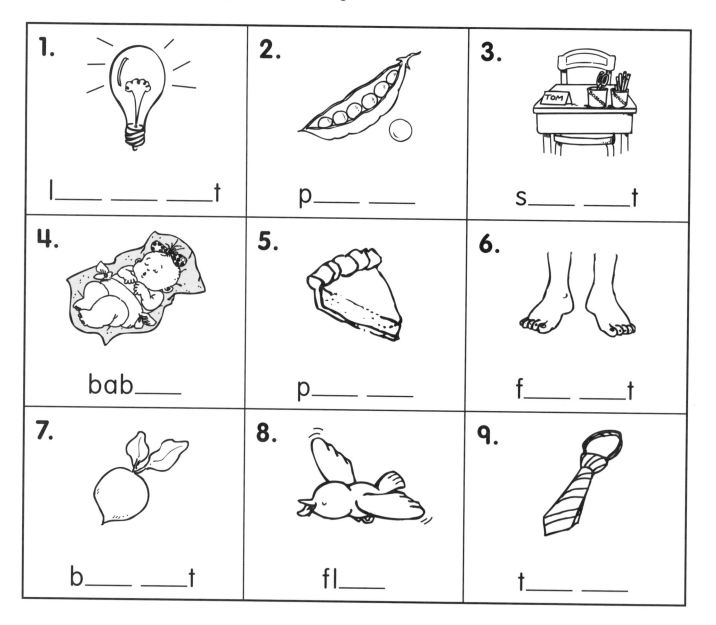

1. l___ ___ ___t

2. p___ ___

3. s___ ___t

4. bab___

5. p___ ___

6. f___ ___t

7. b___ ___t

8. fl___

9. t___ ___

Review: Long vowel digraphs ea, ee, ie, igh, e and i sounds of y

Name _____

Sort It!

Say each word. Listen to the vowel sound.
Write the word in the correct box.

ē	ī

Word Box

by	sunny	pie	high
team	sight	sky	greet
light	bee	meal	tree

Review: long vowel digraphs **ea**, **ee**, **ie**, **igh**, **e** and **i** sounds of **y**

Make Sense of It!

Choose words from the word box to
complete each sentence.
Cross out each word after you use it.

1. The tasty _____ was _____.

What a good _____!

2. Hold on _____.

This ride may give you a _____!

3. He did not _____ on the _____ car.

4. Will she _____ when you say _____?

5. She told a _____ joke about a

_____. It wanted to _____.

Word Box

fright	meal	puppy	fly
funny	cry	clean	good-bye
tight	free	deal	lean

Review: Long vowel digraphs ea, ee, ie, igh, e and i sounds of y

Name _____

A Story to Read

Circle the **long e** spellings: **ea**, **ee**, **y**.
Draw a line under the **long i** spellings: **ie**, **igh**, **y**.

A Fright from the Sky

Mother Bunny needed to hunt for greens to eat.

"Lie here, Baby Bunny. Do not leave the nest," said Mother. "You might meet something that will give you a fright."

Baby Bunny did not mind. He wanted to see all the neat sights.

"My, this is great fun," he said as he hopped along.

A great bird fell from the sky. It tried to pick up Baby Bunny. Just in time, Baby Bunny dove under a log.

"That was not funny," he said. "Mom was right. That sight did give me a fright. I had better go home. Soon it will be night."

Review: Long vowel digraphs ea, ee, ie, igh, and sounds of y

Spell It!

| ai ay oa oe ow ue ui oo |

Say the name of each picture.
Choose the correct spelling for the missing letters.

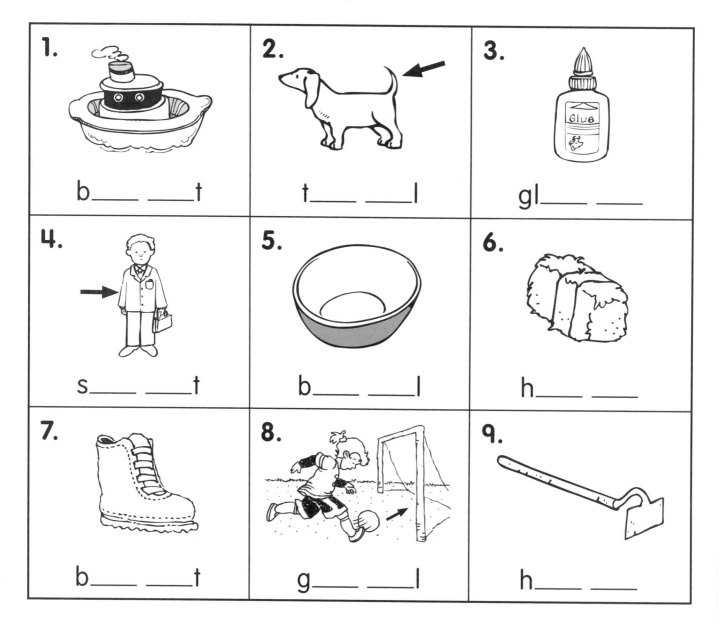

1. b____ ____t	2. t____ ____l	3. gl____ ____
4. s____ ____t	5. b____ ____l	6. h____ ____
7. b____ ____t	8. g____ ____l	9. h____ ____

Review: Long vowel digraphs ai, ay, oa, oe, ow, ue, ui, oo

Name _____

Sort It!

Say each word. Listen to the vowel sound.
Write the word in the correct box.

ā	ō	o͞o

Word Box

grain	afraid	wait	moan	trail	loon
toes	suit	float	clue	blow	clay
spoon	woe	hoot	flow	fruit	pray

Review: Long vowel digraphs ai, ay, oa, oe, ow, ue, ui, oo

Make Sense of It!

Choose words from the word box to complete each sentence.

1. Please _____ here.

   Wait for the _____ by the tracks.

2. The wind will _____ the _____ away.

3. Can you _____ the weeds by the

   _____ trees?

4. The _____ _____ its horn.

   It will stop at the dock _____.

5. He put on his _____ _____ for
   the party.

Word Box

stay	boat	hoe	fruit
toots	rain	soon	blue
suit	train	blow	

Review: Long vowel digraphs **ai, ay, oa, oe, ow, ue, ui, oo**

Name _____

A Story to Read

Circle the **long a** spellings: **ai**, **ay**.
Draw a line under the **long o** spellings: **oa**, **ow**.
X the **oo** spellings: **ue**, **ui**, **oo**.

Blue Goose

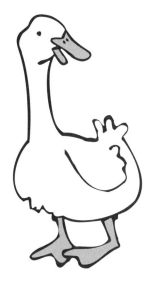

Blue Goose lived beside the
bay. Winter did not suit him at all.

"I do not like snow," he said.
"I do not wish to be blue! I cannot
stay here. I'd like to roam. I will fly
far from here soon."

Blue Goose didn't have to fly far. He saw
a boat that was sailing out of the bay.

"I will stow away on that floating thing,"
he said.

And so he did.

Review: Long vowel digraphs ai, ay, oa, ow, ue, ui, oo

Name _____

Spell It!

Circle the word that names the picture.

1.		tight	dime	tie
2.		tie	pie	time
3.		we	tea	pea
4.		tow	bow	boat
5.		flute	suit	fruit
6.		boat	bow	bone
7.		tape	lay	tail
8.		me	bee	tea
9.		hay	ate	hail

Review: All long vowel spelling patterns

Name _____

Make Sense of It!

Choose words from the word box to fill in each blank.

1. I tripped on the tree _____ and hurt my
   _____.

2. In the _____, we can see
   the _____ sail by.

3. Wash the dirty _____ with the dish
   _____.

4. I _____ wear a _____ to the party.

5. Will the fish think the _____ is a
   _____?

Word Box

treat	tray	toe	might	tie
root	daylight	soap	bait	fleet

Review: All long vowel spelling patterns

Name _____

Circle all the words in the story that have a long vowel sound.

A **Fun** **Night**

I planned to meet my friend Sue at the show at 7:00 last night. We would both wear blue caps so that we could find each other. We ate fruit loops.

At the end, we got up to leave. I forgot my coat.

"May I go back in?" I asked the man in the suit.

"Duck low. Don't block the show," he said.

Write each long vowel word in the correct box.

ā	ē	ī	ō	o͞o
A		night		

Review: All long vowel spelling patterns

Beginning & Ending Consonant Blends

BASIC Phonics Skills

Blend It

Phonics Fact!

2 consonants together that can both be heard
are called a **consonant blend**.

s + t = st

Say the name of each picture.
Listen for the beginning blend.
Draw a line to another picture that begins with that blend.
Write the sounds you hear on the lines.

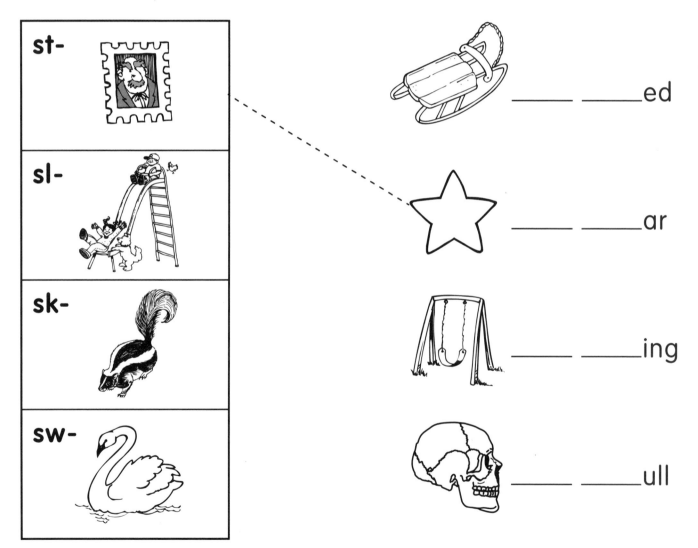

st-

sl-

sk-

sw-

_____ _____ed

_____ _____ar

_____ _____ing

_____ _____ull

Distinguishing among beginning consonant blends: st, sl, sk, sw

Consonant Blends

Fill in the circle by the sound you hear at the beginning of each word.

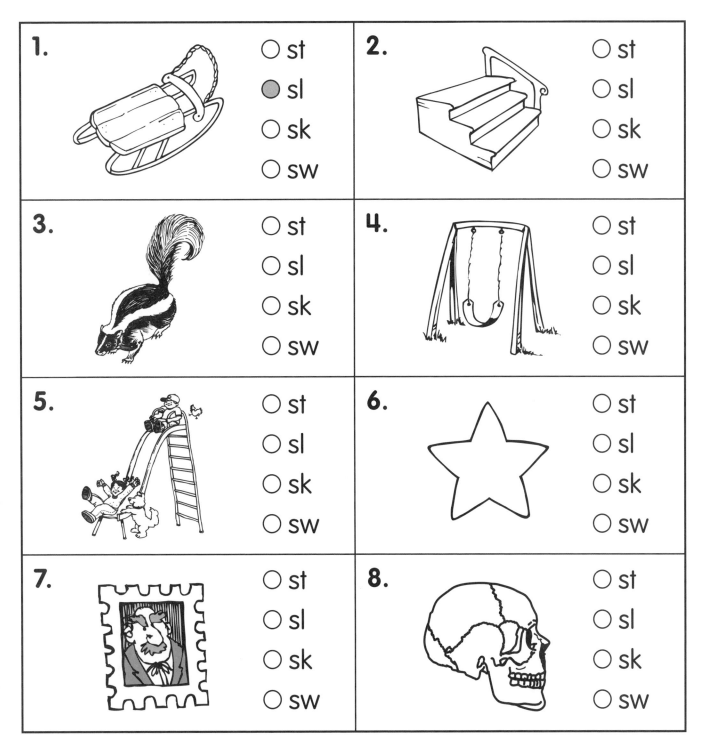

1.
- ○ st
- ● sl
- ○ sk
- ○ sw

2.
- ○ st
- ○ sl
- ○ sk
- ○ sw

3.
- ○ st
- ○ sl
- ○ sk
- ○ sw

4.
- ○ st
- ○ sl
- ○ sk
- ○ sw

5.
- ○ st
- ○ sl
- ○ sk
- ○ sw

6.
- ○ st
- ○ sl
- ○ sk
- ○ sw

7.
- ○ st
- ○ sl
- ○ sk
- ○ sw

8.
- ○ st
- ○ sl
- ○ sk
- ○ sw

Distinguishing among beginning consonant blends: st, sl, sk, sw

| st | sl | sk | sw |

Name the picture.
Listen to the sounds.
Fill in the missing letters.

1.  ___ ___ove	**2.**  ___ ___im	**3.**  ___ ___unk
4.  ___ ___ide	**5.**  ___ ___ates	**6.**  ___ ___op
7. 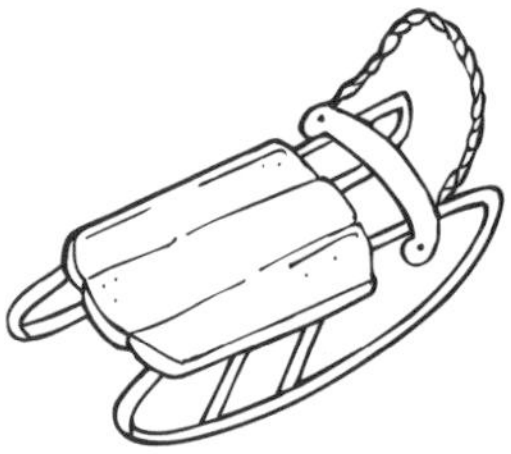 ___ ___ed	**8.**  ___ ___an	**9.** 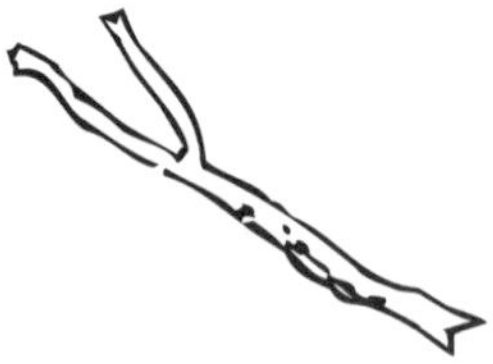 ___ ___ick

Distinguishing among beginning consonant blends: st, sl, sk, sw

Name _____

Write the Word

Say the name of each picture.
Write it on the line.

Swing up to the sky.

1. _____

2. _____

3. _____

4. _____

5. _____

6. _____

Word Box

skull	stone	sweep	state	sweet
swim	sled	sky	stop	stick

Writing words with beginning s blends

Read Blends
st sl sk sw

Circle the word that best completes
each sentence.

1. I need a _____ for the letter.

  swing   **skin**   **stamp**

2. The _____ is hot.

  ski   **stove**   **sweep**

3. The _____ is in the lake.

  swan   **slap**   **stay**

4. That _____ is high in the sky.

  swim   **step**   **star**

5. The _____ is clear tonight.

  slip   **sky**   **sweet**

6. The _____ is open.

  store   **swim**   **slam**

7. I will _____ the floor.

  slope   **sweep**   **skin**

8. I climbed up the _____.

  slip   **stem**   **steps**

Completing sentences with s-blend words

Blend It

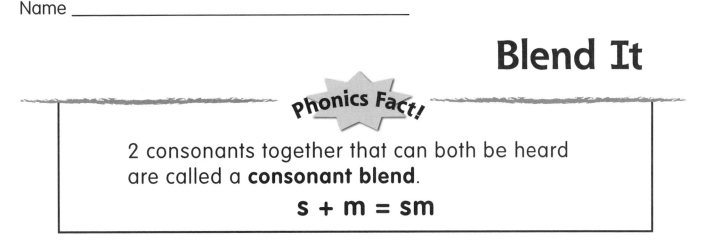

Phonics Fact!

2 consonants together that can both be heard are called a **consonant blend**.

s + m = sm

Say the name of each picture.
Listen for the beginning blend.
Draw a line to another picture that begins with that blend.
Write the sounds you hear on the lines.

sm-

sn-

sp-

sc-

____ ____ail

____ ____oon

____ ____oke

____ ____are

Distinguishing among beginning **s** blends: **sm, sn, sp, sc**

Name _____

Consonant Blends

Say the name of each picture.
Fill in the circle by the sound you hear at the beginning.

1. ○ sm ● sn ○ sp ○ sc

2. ○ sm ○ sn ○ sp ○ sc

3. ○ sm ○ sn ○ sp ○ sc

4. ○ sm ○ sn ○ sp ○ sc

5. ○ sm ○ sn ○ sp ○ sc

6. ○ sm ○ sn ○ sp ○ sc

7. ○ sm ○ sn ○ sp ○ sc

8. ○ sm ○ sn ○ sp ○ sc

Distinguishing among beginning s blends: sm, sn, sp, sc

Basic Phonics Skills, Level C • EMC 3320 • ©2004 by Evan-Moor Corp.

Name _____

Listen for Blends

sm	**sn**	**sp**	**sc**

Name the picture.
Listen to the sounds.
Fill in the missing letters.

1. ___ ___ace

2. ___ ___ool

3. ___ ___ap

4. ___ ___ile

5. ___ ___ail

6. ___ ___ale

7. ___ ___ill

8. ___ ___ake

9. ___ ___oop

Writing words with beginning **s** blends

Write the Word

Say the name of each picture.
Write it on the line.

1.

2.

3.

4.

5.

6.

7.

8.

9.

Word Box

smoke	scare	snap	spoon	spot
snake	spill	spider	snail	scoop

Writing words with beginning s blends

Beginning & Ending Consonant Blends   Basic Phonics Skills, Level C • EMC 3320 • ©2004 by Evan-Moor Corp.

Name _____

Read Blends

Circle the word that best completes
each sentence.

1. I need a _____ for my soup.

    swim   **snow**   **spoon**

2. Our game had a high _____.

    smell   **score**   **spill**

3. The _____ made a web.

    sneeze   **spider**   **scare**

4. It might _____ today.

    snow   **small**   **sweet**

5. There are stars in _____.

    space   **snip**   **score**

6. That food _____ good.

    scale   **snail**   **smells**

7. This _____ is slow.

    snail   **smell**   **score**

8. He has a nice _____.

    sweep   **scare**   **smile**

Completing sentences with s-blend words

Name _____

Blends Review

Look at each picture.
Read the sentences.
Copy the one that tells about the picture.

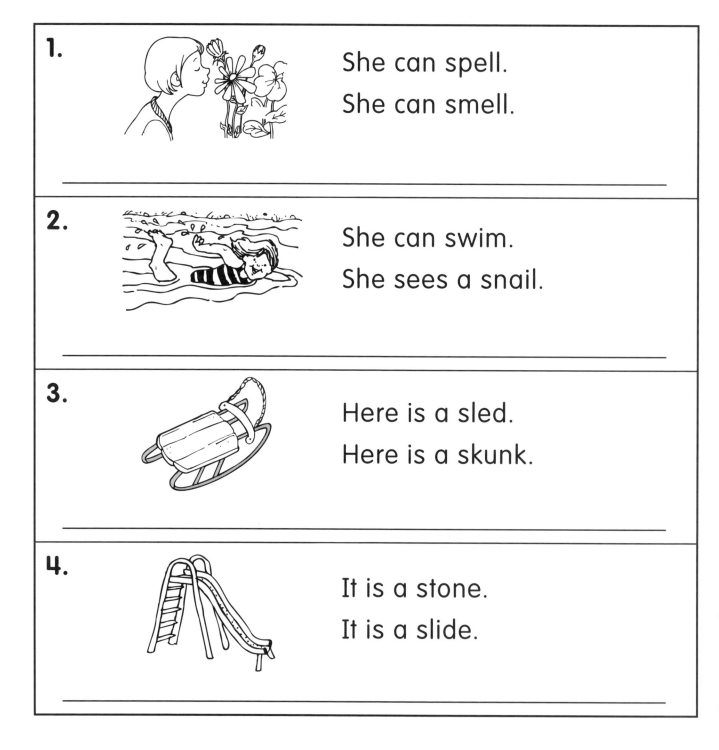

1.

She can spell.

She can smell.

_____

2.

She can swim.

She sees a snail.

_____

3.

Here is a sled.

Here is a skunk.

_____

4.

It is a stone.

It is a slide.

_____

Review: Beginning s blends

Name _____

**st sl sk sw
sm sn sp sc**

Write the word that completes
each sentence.

1. I saw a snake on the _____.

    swim   **steps**   **slam**

2. I smell _____.

    smile   **stamp**   **smoke**

3. He will sled on the _____.

    smoke   **snow**   **still**

4. Did the fox _____ you?

    scare   **swim**   **ski**

5. The _____ smells bad.

    sweet   **speed**   **skunk**

6. Did he _____ the milk?

    sleep   **spill**   **stem**

7. Don't _____ on the ice.

    slip   **star**   **swim**

8. A _____ swims in our lake.

    snow   **slug**   **swan**

Review: Beginning s blends

Name _____

Blend It

Phonics Fact!

2 consonants together that can both be heard
are called a **consonant blend**.

f + l = fl

Say the name of each picture.
Listen for the beginning blend.
Draw a line to another picture that begins with that blend.
Write the sounds you hear on the lines.

fl-

cl-

gl-

_____ _____own

_____ _____obe

_____ _____y

_____ _____ue

Distinguishing among beginning l blends: fl, cl, gl

Basic Phonics Skills, Level C • EMC 3320 • ©2004 by Evan-Moor Corp.

Consonant Blends

Fill in the circle by the sound you hear at the beginning of each word.

1.
○ fl
○ cl
○ gl

2.
○ fl
○ cl
○ gl

3.
○ fl
○ cl
○ gl

4.
○ fl
○ cl
○ gl

5.
○ fl
○ cl
○ gl

6.
○ fl
○ cl
○ gl

7.
○ fl
○ cl
○ gl

8.
○ fl
○ cl
○ gl

Distinguishing among beginning l blends: fl, cl, gl

Listen for Blends

fl	cl	gl

Name the picture.
Listen to the sounds.
Fill in the missing letters.

1. ____ ____own

2. ____ ____ue

3. ____ ____ute

4. ____ ____ap

5. ____ ____ock

6. ____ ____ass

7. ____ ____ag

8. ____ ____oud

9. ____ ____ove

Writing words with beginning l blends: fl, cl, gl

Name _____

Write the Word

Say the name of each picture.
Write the word on the line.

1. _____

2. _____

3. _____

4. _____

5. _____

6. _____

7. _____

8. _____

9. _____

Word Box

glad	glue	globe	clap	flag
flame	flute	clown	float	clock

Writing words with beginning l blends: **fl, cl, gl**

Name _____

Clara the Clown

Circle the word that best completes
each sentence.

1. The _____ was funny.

    glass   **clown**   **float**

2. She played the _____.

    glue   **clock**   **flute**

3. She had white _____.

    gloves   **flip**   **club**

4. She came to our _____.

    glass   **class**   **floss**

5. She waved a _____.

    glow   **flag**   **clam**

6. It was a _____ day.

    cloudy   **glass**   **flower**

7. She danced across the _____.

    floor   **clock**   **glass**

8. We were all _____ she came.

    flat   **glad**   **clap**

Completing sentences with l-blend words

Name _____

Blend It

2 consonants together that can both be heard
are called a **consonant blend**.

p + l = pl   b + l = bl

Say the name of each picture.
Listen for the beginning blend.
Draw a line to another picture that begins with that blend.
Write the sounds you hear on the lines.

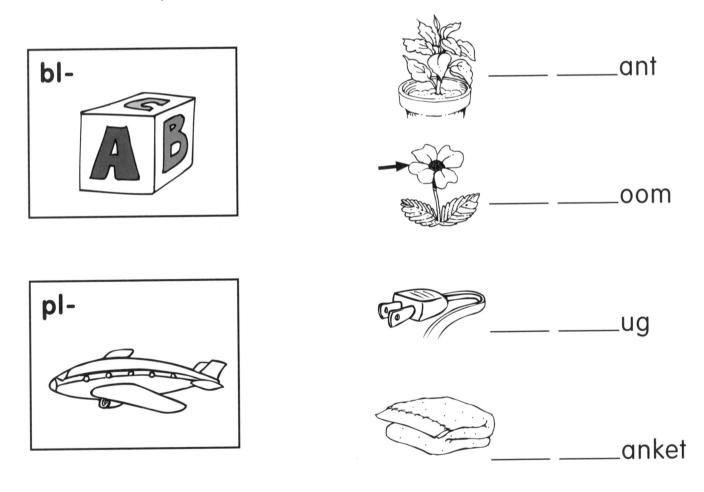

bl-

pl-

_____ _____ant

_____ _____oom

_____ _____ug

_____ _____anket

Distinguishing among beginning l blends: **bl, pl**

Listen for Blends

gl	pl	bl

Name the picture.
Listen to the sounds.
Fill in the missing letters.

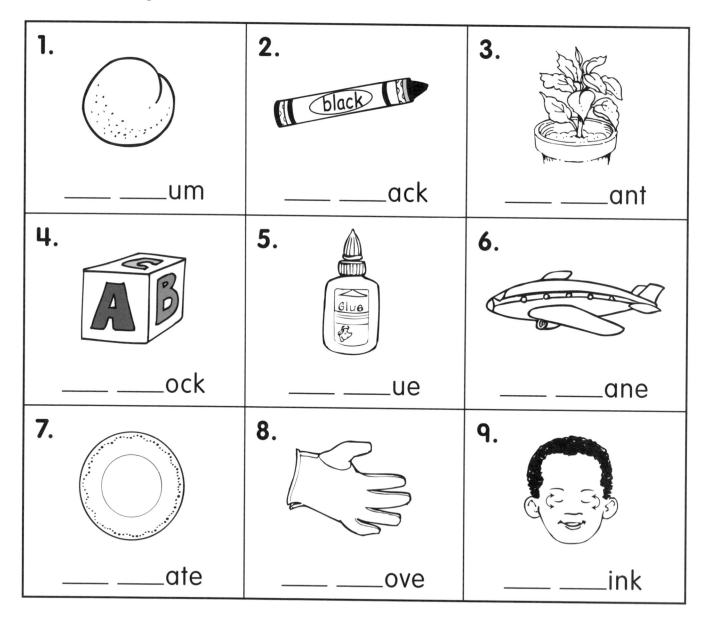

1. ___ ___um

2. black ___ ___ack

3. ___ ___ant

4. ___ ___ock

5. Glue ___ ___ue

6. ___ ___ane

7. ___ ___ate

8. ___ ___ove

9. ___ ___ink

Writing words with beginning l blends: **bl, gl, pl**

Name _____

Blends Plus "Ends"

Make new words by changing beginning consonant blends.

| fl | cl | gl | bl | pl |

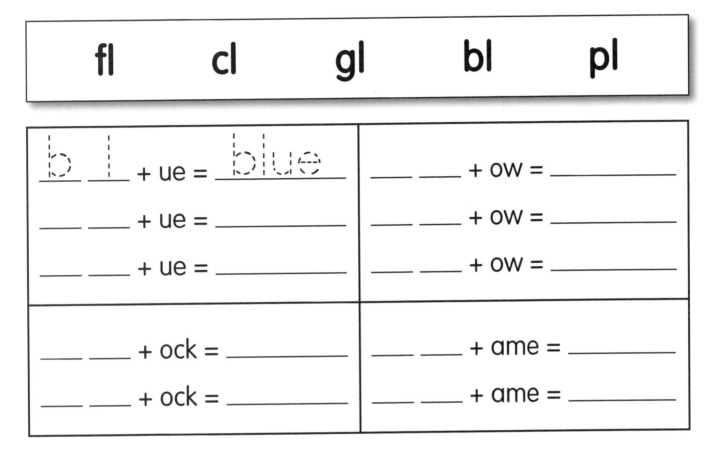

b l + ue = blue

____ ____ + ue = _____

____ ____ + ue = _____

____ ____ + ow = _____

____ ____ + ow = _____

____ ____ + ow = _____

____ ____ + ock = _____

____ ____ + ock = _____

____ ____ + ame = _____

____ ____ + ame = _____

Write a sentence using the two words.

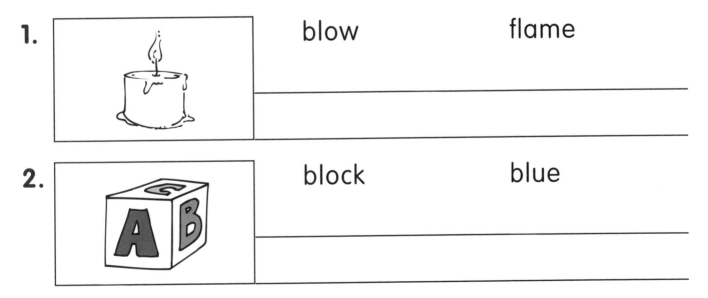

1.   blow   flame

_____

2.   block   blue

_____

Writing words with beginning l blends

Name _____

Write the Word

Bloom, bloom, little plant.

Say the name of each picture.
Write it on the line.

1. _____

2. _____

3. _____

4. _____

5. _____

6. _____

Word Box

plant	plow	blade	block	play
please	plug	blame	blow	bloom

Writing words with beginning l blends: **bl, pl**

144 **Beginning & Ending Consonant Blends**

Basic Phonics Skills, Level C • EMC 3320 • ©2004 by Evan-Moor Corp.

Read Blends

bl pl

Circle the word that best completes the sentence.

1. The _____ is big.

    blue   **plant**   **plus**

2. The baby plays with a _____.

    block   **place**   **plow**

3. The _____ flew high above.

    block   **plane**   **bleed**

4. Mars is a _____.

    black   **blade**   **planet**

5. The _____ was sweet.

    plum   **bleed**   **block**

6. The sky was _____.

    plate   **plug**   **blue**

7. The wind can _____ hard.

    plow   **blow**   **blade**

8. The night sky is _____.

    black   **plus**   **plum**

Completing sentences with beginning l blends: **bl, pl**

Blends Review
fl cl gl bl pl

Look at each picture.
Read the sentences.
Copy the one that tells about the picture.

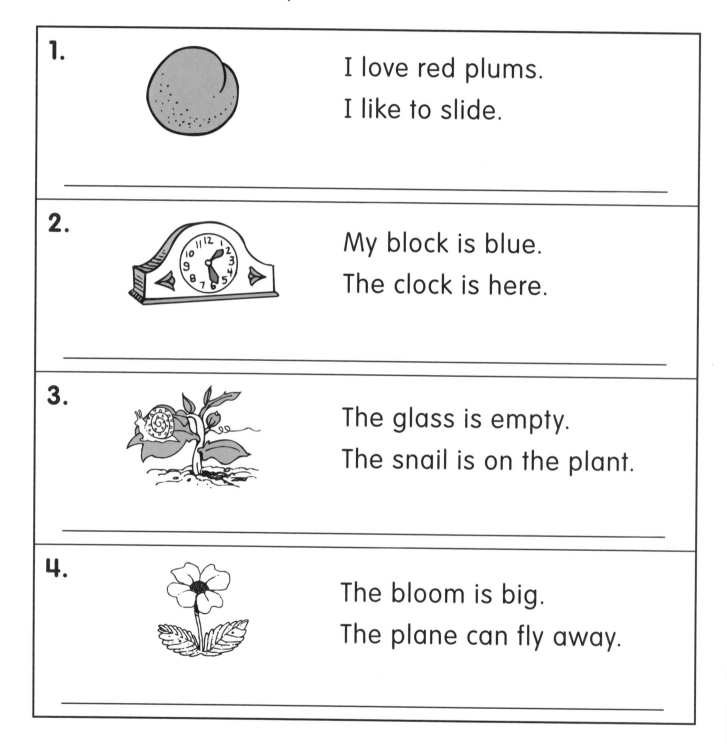

1.

I love red plums.

I like to slide.

_____

2.

My block is blue.

The clock is here.

_____

3.

The glass is empty.

The snail is on the plant.

_____

4.

The bloom is big.

The plane can fly away.

_____

Review: Reading words with beginning l blends

Name _____

Blends Review

Write the word that completes
each sentence.

1. The _____ will blow up balloons.

    flow   **clown**   **float**

2. Don't _____ with the sharp blade.

    blue   **glove**   **play**

3. The ocean is very _____ today.

    clue   **flew**   **blue**

4. The _____ is red, white, and blue.

    flag   **black**   **clock**

5. The snail ate my _____.

    plate   **plant**   **flow**

6. Look at the stars on a _____ night.

    plum   **glow**   **clear**

7. I like milk in that _____.

    fled   **glass**   **glue**

8. "Tick, tock" says the _____.

    clue   **clown**   **clock**

Review: Completing sentences with l-blend words

Name _____

Blend It

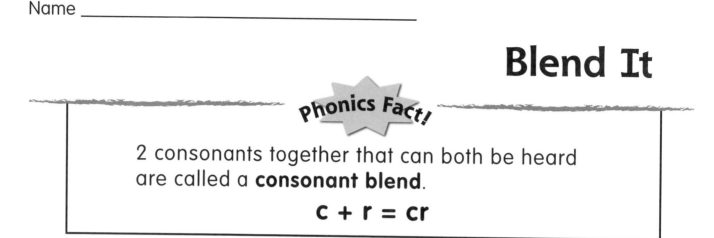

2 consonants together that can both be heard
are called a **consonant blend**.

c + r = cr

Say the name of each picture.
Listen for the beginning blend.
Draw a line to another picture that begins with that blend.
Write the sounds you hear on the lines.

cr-

fr-

gr-

_____ _____apes

_____ _____ow

_____ _____ame

_____ _____ab

Distinguishing among beginning r blends: cr, fr, gr

Basic Phonics Skills, Level C • EMC 3320 • ©2004 by Evan-Moor Corp.

Name _____

Consonant Blends

Fill in the circle by the sound you hear at the beginning of each word.

1. ○ cr ○ fr ○ gr

2. ○ cr ○ fr ○ gr

3. ○ cr ○ fr ○ gr

4. ○ cr ○ fr ○ gr

5. ○ cr ○ fr ○ gr

6. ○ cr ○ fr ○ gr

7. ○ cr ○ fr ○ gr

8. ○ cr ○ fr ○ gr

Distinguishing among beginning r blends: cr, fr, gr

©2004 by Evan-Moor Corp. • Basic Phonics Skills, Level C • EMC 3320

Beginning & Ending
Consonant Blends   149

Listen for Blends

cr	fr	gr

Name the picture.
Listen to the sounds.
Fill in the missing letters.

1. ___ ___ow

2. ___ ___og

3. ___ ___ame

4. ___ ___apes

5. ___ ___uit

6. ___ ___ay

7. ___ ___ill

8. ___ ___ab

9. ___ ___oss

Writing words with beginning r blends: **cr, fr, gr**

Name _____

Write the Word

Say the name of each picture.
Write it on the line.

1.	2.	3.
grin		
4.	5.	6.
7.	8.	9.

Word Box

grill	crawl	frame	frown	crown
fruit	grass	cross	grin	crow

Writing words with beginning r blends: **cr, fr, gr**

Name _____

Circle the word that best completes
each sentence.

1. The _____ was black.

    flow   **crow**   **grow**

2. The tree will _____ tall.

    crow   **grow**   **flow**

3. Greg will _____ the road.

    frost   **gloss**   **cross**

4. Fred will not _____.

    cry   **greed**   **fry**

5. The man has a _____ on his head.

    grown   **frown**   **crown**

6. She has a gold _____.

    frame   **gray**   **cry**

7. The _____ flows fast.

    free   **greed**   **creek**

8. I got a note _____ Grace.

    grin   **from**   **crop**

Completing sentences with r-blend words

Blend It

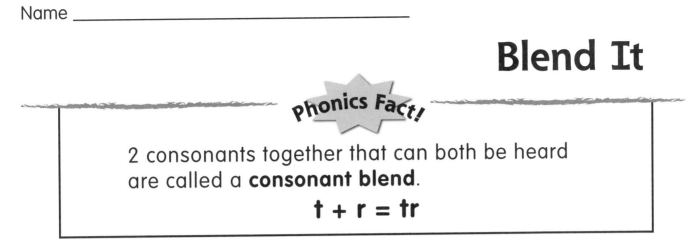

Phonics Fact!

2 consonants together that can both be heard
are called a **consonant blend**.

t + r = tr

Say the name of each picture.
Listen for the beginning blend.
Draw a line to another picture that begins with that blend.
Write the sounds you hear on the lines.

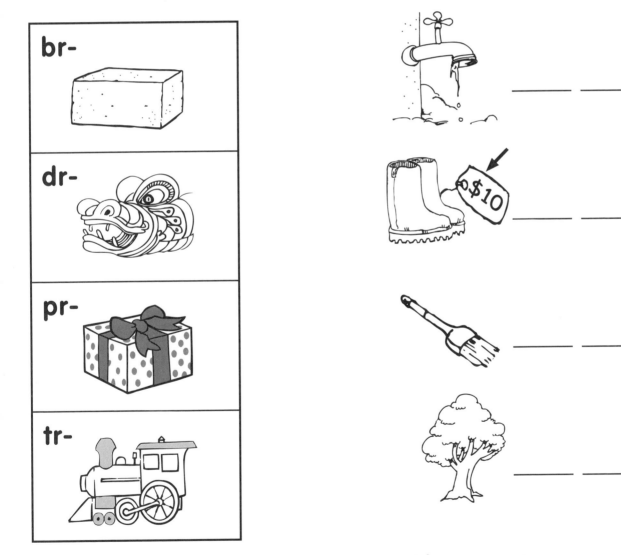

br-

dr-

pr-

tr-

_____ _____ip

_____ _____ice

_____ _____ush

_____ _____ee

Distinguishing among beginning r blends: br, dr, pr, tr

Consonant Blends

Fill in the circle by the sound you hear
at the beginning of each word.

1. ● br ○ dr ○ pr ○ tr	**2.** ○ br ○ dr ○ pr ○ tr
3. ○ br ○ dr ○ pr ○ tr	**4.** ○ br ○ dr ○ pr ○ tr
5. ○ br ○ dr ○ pr ○ tr	**6.** ○ br ○ dr ○ pr ○ tr
7. ○ br ○ dr ○ pr ○ tr	**8.** ○ br ○ dr ○ pr ○ tr

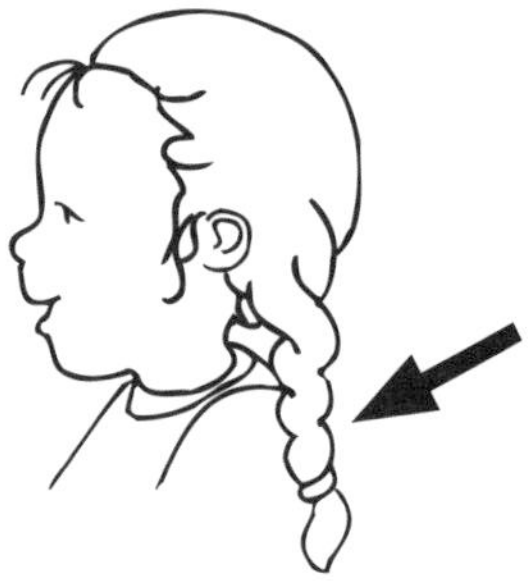

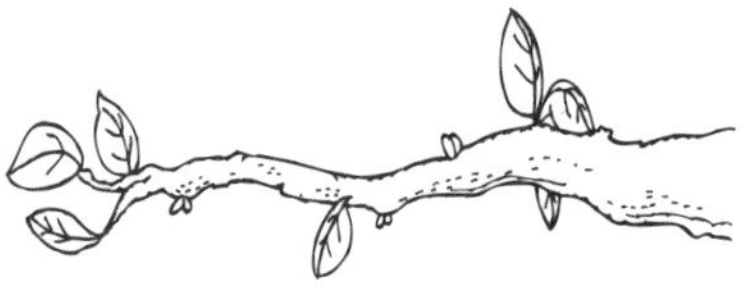

Distinguishing among beginning r blends: br, dr, pr, tr

Name _____

Listen for Blends

br	dr	pr	tr

Name the picture.
Listen to the sounds.
Fill in the missing letters.

1. ____ ____uck

2. ____ ____ink

3. ____ ____ee

4. ____ ____um

5. ____ ____aid

6. ____ ____ize

7. ____ ____ick

8. ____ ____esent

9. ____ ____ay

Writing words with beginning r blends: br, dr, pr, tr

Name _____

Write the Word

Say the name of each picture.
Write it on the line.

The truck drops off the bricks.

1. _____

2. _____

3. _____

4. _____

5. _____

6. _____

Word Box

bread	prize	dragon	truck	drill
prune	trash	bridge	dress	drum

Writing words with beginning r blends: **br, dr, pr, tr**

Basic Phonics Skills, Level C • EMC 3320 • ©2004 by Evan-Moor Corp.

Name _____

Read Blends

Circle the word that best completes
each sentence.

1. Ben rode on a _____.
  brain   **train**   **drain**

2. I ate a dried _____.
  true   **drew**   **prune**

3. Beat that _____!
  drum   **brown**   **pretty**

4. Mother had to _____ the napkins.
  brass   **dress**   **press**

5. Pam won the _____.
  prize   **drive**   **drain**

6. Drew sat under a _____.
  drum   **pride**   **tree**

7. He _____ a cat.
  drew   **proof**   **true**

8. She had a new _____ for the party.
  press   **brass**   **dress**

Completing sentences with **r-blend** words

Name _____

Blends Review

Look at each picture. Read the sentences.
Copy the one that tells about the picture.

1. The truck stopped.

The train zoomed.

_____

2. The brick broke.

The dress is pretty.

_____

3. The queen has a crown.

She won the prize.

_____

4. She has one braid.

The bread is brown.

_____

Review: Reading words with beginning r blends

Basic Phonics Skills, Level C • EMC 3320 • ©2004 by Evan-Moor Corp.

Blends Review

cr fr gr
br dr pr tr

Write the word that completes each sentence.

1. The house is made of _____.

    pride   **brick**   **fry**

2. The _____ needs to be cut.

    press   **grass**   **brass**

3. We took a _____ on a train.

    trip   **brim**   **drip**

4. Fran wore a green _____.

    brass   **press**   **dress**

5. Fred eats a lot of _____.

    frames   **grapes**   **trails**

6. She saw a big green _____.

    bride   **trot**   **frog**

7. Baby, please don't _____.

    dry   **cry**   **try**

8. The paint is _____.

    dry   **cry**   **try**

Review: Completing sentences with beginning r blends

Match It

Say the name of each picture.
Listen for the beginning blend.
Draw a line to another picture that begins with that blend.
Write the sounds you hear on the lines.

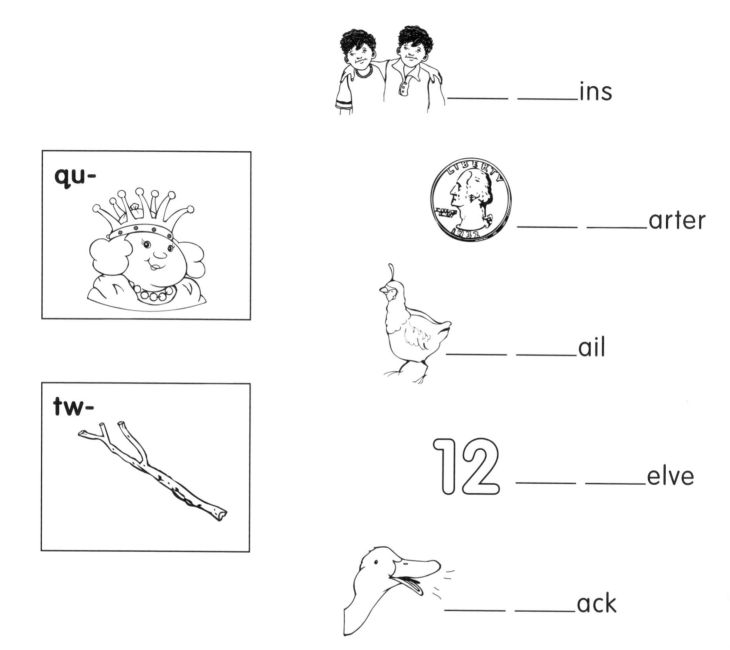

qu-

tw-

_____ _____ins

_____ _____arter

_____ _____ail

12 _____ _____elve

_____ _____ack

Distinguishing among words that begin with consonant clusters qu and tw

Name _____

Listen

Fill in the circle by the correct beginning sound.

1.
20
○ qu
○ tw

2.
○ qu
○ tw

3.
○ qu
○ tw

4.
○ qu
○ tw

5.
○ qu
○ tw

6.
12
○ qu
○ tw

7.
○ qu
○ tw

8.
○ qu
○ tw

Distinguishing among words that begin with consonant clusters qu and tw

Beginning & Ending Consonant Blends **161**

Write the Word

Say the name of each picture.
Write the word on the line.

1. _____

2. _____

3. _____

4. _____

5. _____

6. _____

7. _____

8. _____

9. _____

Word Box

twig	twins	twelve	quack	quarter
queen	quiet	quail	twenty	quilt

Writing words that begin with consonant clusters qu and tw

Basic Phonics Skills, Level C • EMC 3320 • ©2004 by Evan-Moor Corp.

Review

Circle the word that names the picture.

1.		stamp	star	skunk
2.		snail	smile	snow
3.		slide	skin	sled
4.		fly	flag	glue
5.		glass	clown	globe
6.		block	plane	plant
7.		crow	grow	crown
8.		spill	spoon	smoke

Review: Reading words with beginning consonant blends

Name _____

Write the word that best completes the sentence.

1. The _____ stinks.

   skunk   **sweep**   **stair**

2. The black _____ is on her web.

   spoon   **smile**   **spider**

3. Hear the clock _____ away.

   flame   **click**   **globe**

4. Baby plays with _____.

   blocks   **blooms**   **plates**

5. The queen has a _____.

   brown   **grape**   **crown**

6. The _____ is on the tracks.

   drip   **train**   **tree**

Review: Completing sentences with beginning blend words

Basic Phonics Skills, Level C • EMC 3320 • ©2004 by Evan-Moor Corp.

Blends at the End

Phonics Fact!

2 consonants together that can both be heard
are called a **consonant blend**.

s + t = st

Say the name of each picture.
Listen for the ending blend.
Draw a line to another picture that ends with that blend.
Write the sounds you hear on the lines.

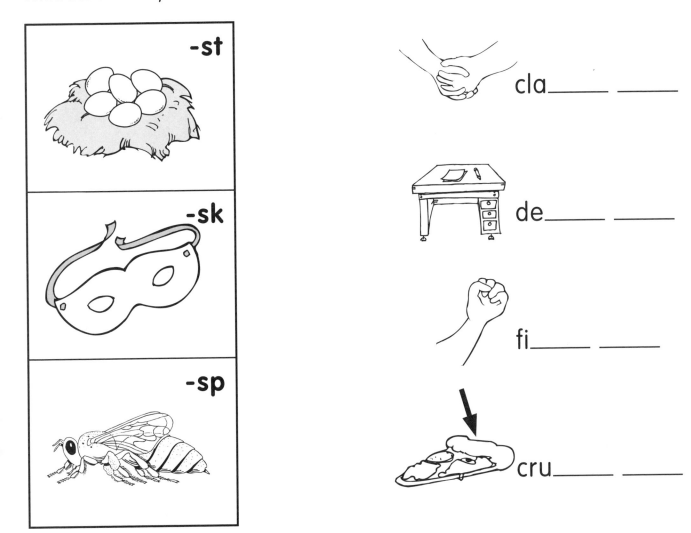

-st

-sk

-sp

cla____ ____

de____ ____

fi____ ____

cru____ ____

Distinguishing among ending blends: st, sk, sp

Name _____

Consonant Blends

Fill in the circle by the sound you hear at the end of each word.

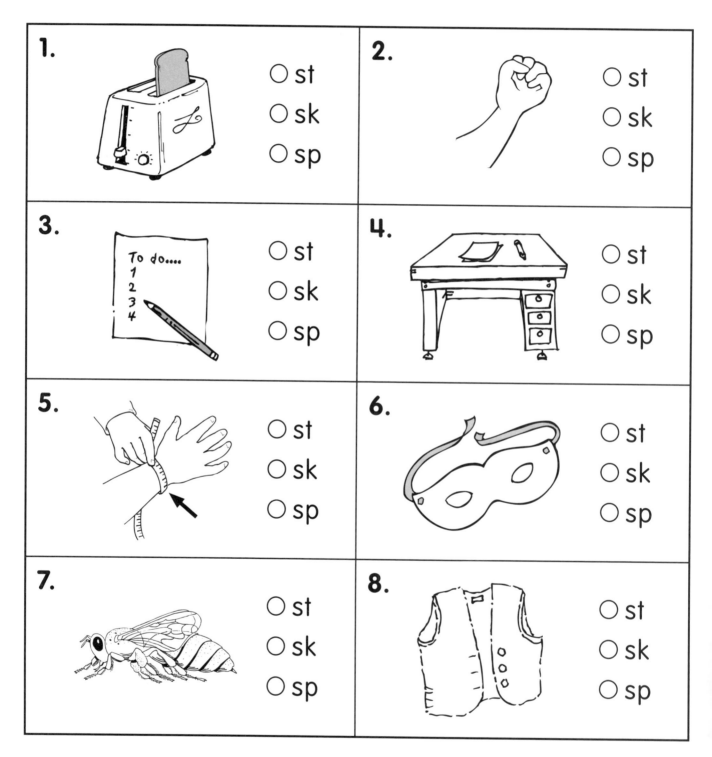

1.
○ st
○ sk
○ sp

2.
○ st
○ sk
○ sp

3.
○ st
○ sk
○ sp

4.
○ st
○ sk
○ sp

5.
○ st
○ sk
○ sp

6.
○ st
○ sk
○ sp

7.
○ st
○ sk
○ sp

8.
○ st
○ sk
○ sp

Distinguishing among ending blends: st, sk, sp

Basic Phonics Skills, Level C • EMC 3320 • ©2004 by Evan-Moor Corp.

Name _____

Name the picture.
Listen to the sounds.
Fill in the missing letters.

| -st | -sk | -sp |

1. ve____ ____

2. wri____ ____

3. de____ ____

4. ne____ ____

5. li____ ____

6. ma____ ____

7. toa____ ____

8. wa____ ____

9. fi____ ____

Writing words with ending blends: **st, sk, sp**

Write the Word

Say the word.
Write it on the line.

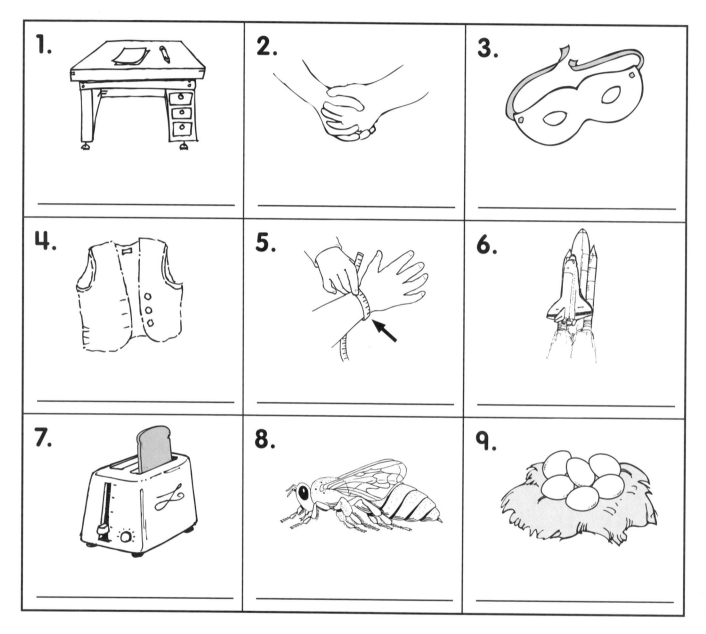

1.

2.

3.

4.

5.

6.

7.

8.

9.

Word Box

wrist	dust	vest	nest	mask
clasp	wasp	toast	blast	desk

Writing words with ending blends: **st, sk, sp**

Consonant Blends at the End

Circle the word that best completes the sentence.

1. The wasp is in its _____.

nest   list   wisp

2. The _____ is in the oven.

mist   roast   grasp

3. The _____ flew onto my desk.

wasp   risk   list

4. I hit the ball with my _____.

mist   fist   nest

5. I put on a _____ for the party.

mast   crisp   mask

6. The _____ on the bread is crisp.

crust   cost   post

7. My _____ is sore from digging.

clasp   wrist   blast

Completing sentences with ending-blend words

Where Do You Hear It?

Fill in the circle to show if you hear the blend at the beginning or the end of each word.

st	→	star	vest
		● ○	○ ●

st

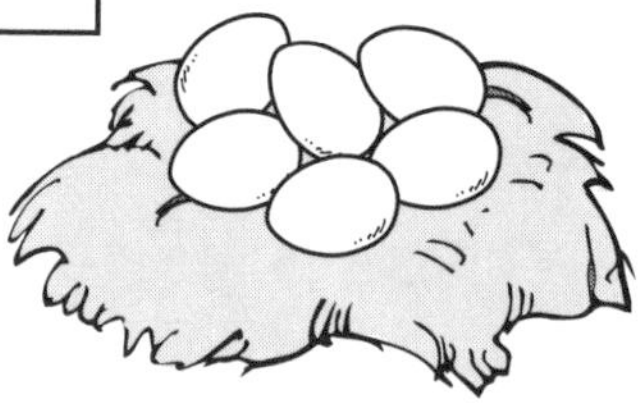

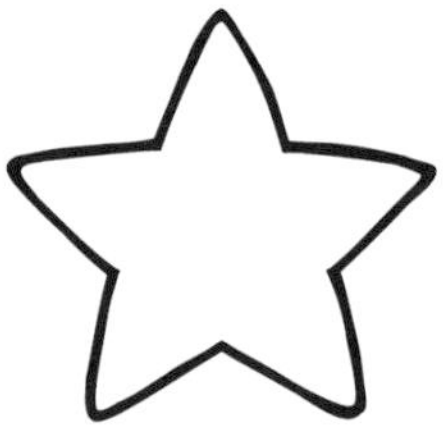

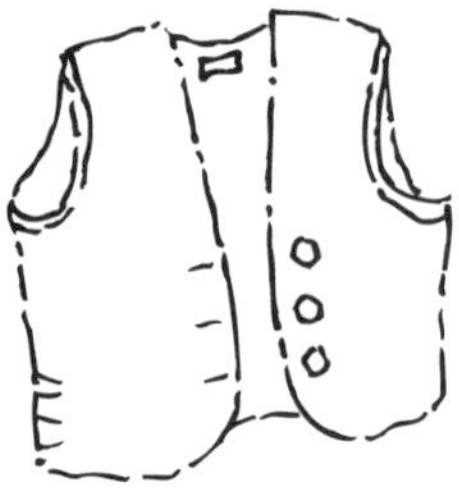

○   ○   ○   ○   ○   ○

sk

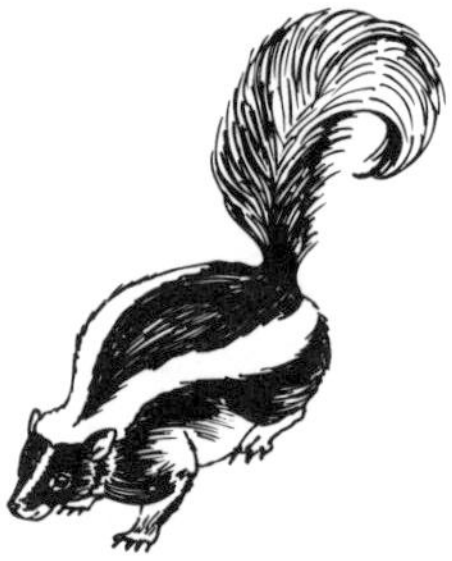

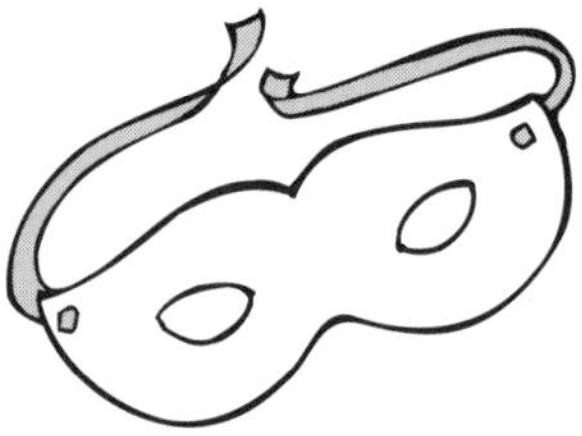

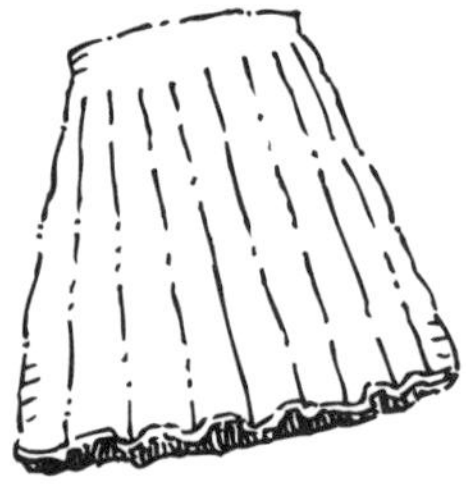

○   ○   ○   ○   ○   ○

sp

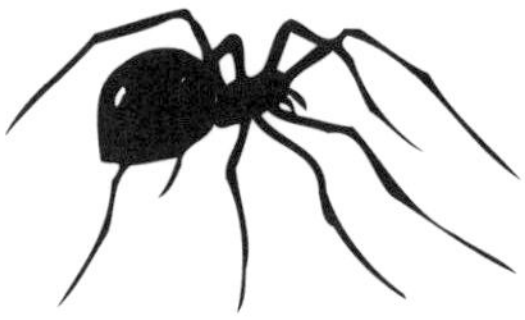

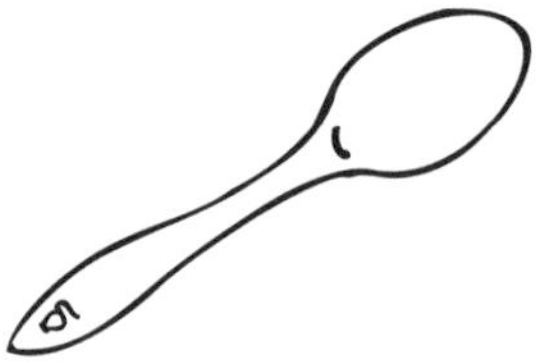

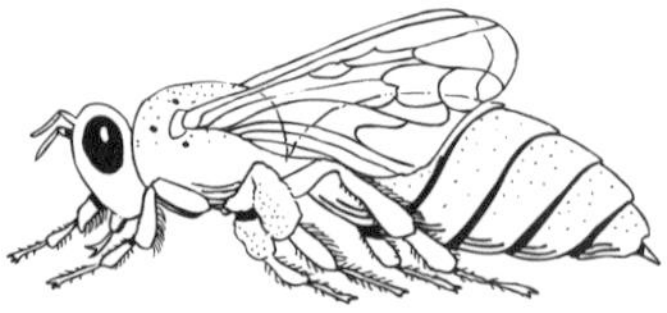

○   ○   ○   ○   ○   ○

Review: Distinguishing among beginning and ending blends: sk, sp, st

Name _____

Circle the picture that correctly shows where you hear each blend.

Beginning	Ending
st-	-st
sk-	-sk
sp-	-sp

Review: Distinguishing among beginning and ending blends: **sk, sp, st**

At the End

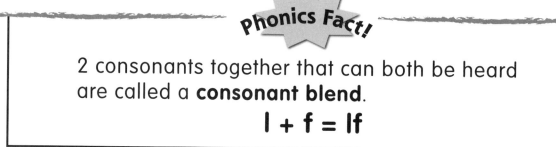

Phonics Fact!

2 consonants together that can both be heard
are called a **consonant blend**.

l + f = lf

Say the name of each picture.
Listen for the ending blend.
Draw a line to another picture that ends with that blend.
Write the sounds you hear on the lines.

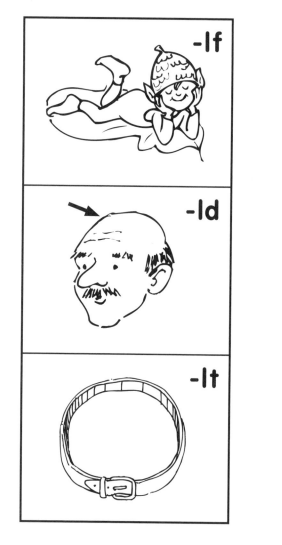

-lf

-ld

-lt

go____ ____

qui____ ____

she____ ____

sa____ ____

Distinguishing among ending blends: lf, ld, lt

Name ________________________________

Consonant Blends

Fill in the circle by the sound you hear at the end of each word.

1.

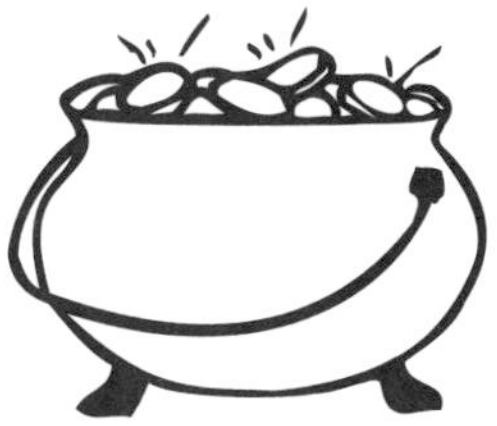

○ lf
○ ld
○ lt

2.

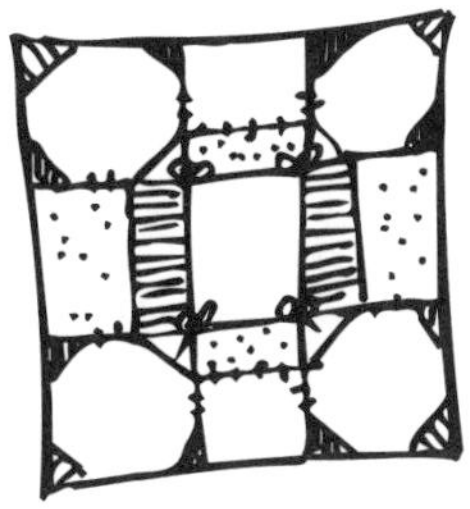

○ lf
○ ld
○ lt

3.

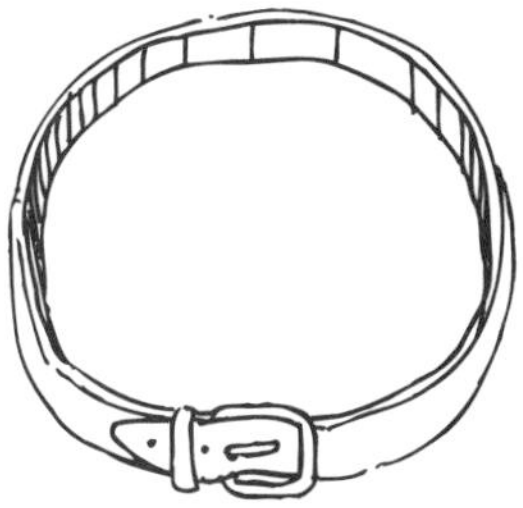

○ lf
○ ld
○ lt

4.

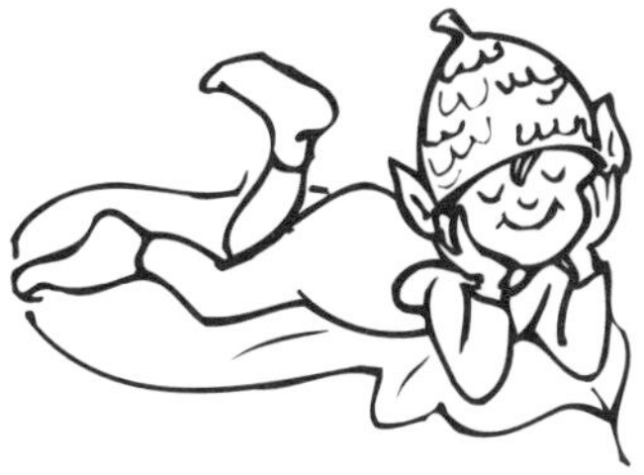

○ lf
○ ld
○ lt

5.

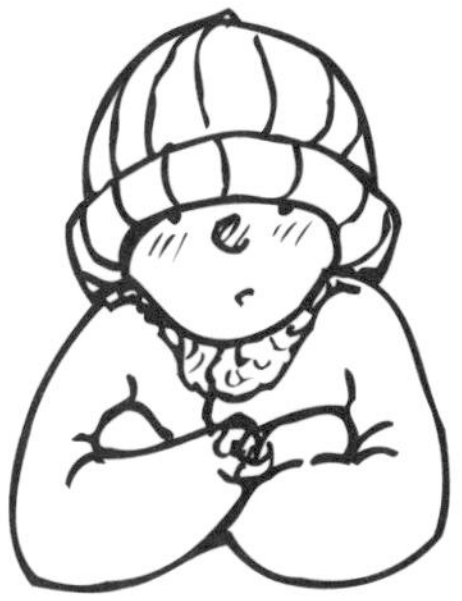

○ lf
○ ld
○ lt

6.

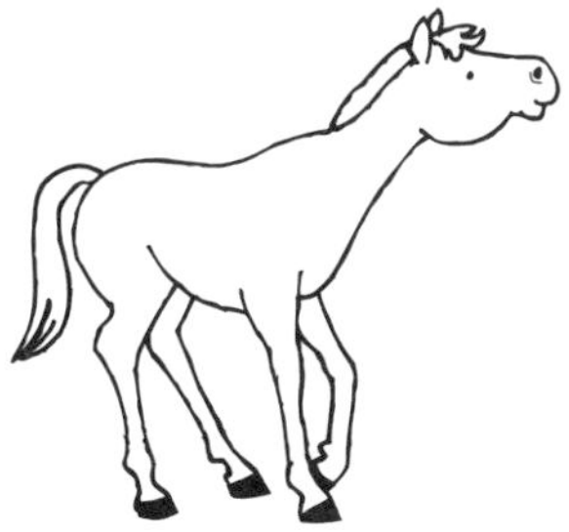

○ lf
○ ld
○ lt

7.

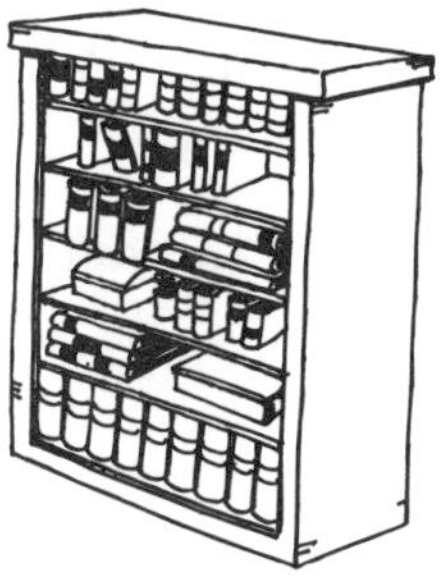

○ lf
○ ld
○ lt

8.

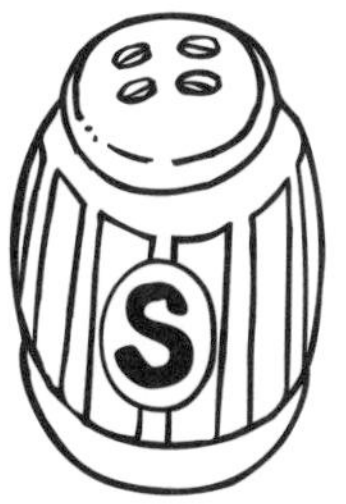

○ lf
○ ld
○ lt

Distinguishing among ending blends: lf, ld, lt

Listen for Blends at the End

Name the picture.
Listen to the sounds at the end.
Fill in the missing letters.

-lf	-ld	-lt

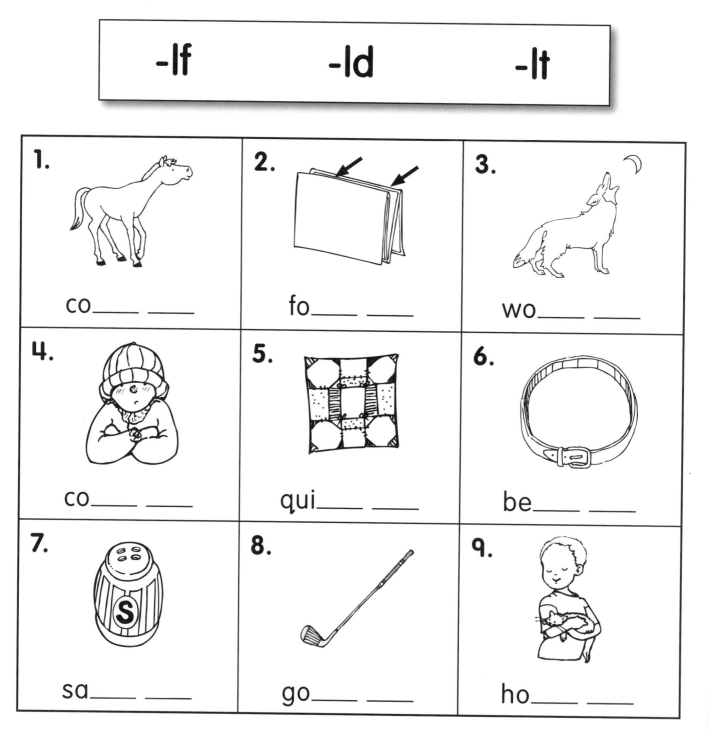

1. co____ ____

2. fo____ ____

3. wo____ ____

4. co____ ____

5. qui____ ____

6. be____ ____

7. sa____ ____

8. go____ ____

9. ho____ ____

Writing words with ending blends: lf, ld, lt

Name _____

Write the Word

-lf   -ld   -lt

Say the name of each picture.
Write it on the line.

1.

2.

3.

4.

5.

6.

Word Box

golf	elf	shelf	salt	belt
gold	quilt	melt	colt	fold

Distinguishing among ending blends: **lf, ld, lt**

Name _____

Read Blends

Circle the word that best completes each sentence.

1. The air was _____ last night.	cold golf
2. Rosa needed her _____.	quilt gold
3. Her mom _____ Rosa she could keep it.	elf told
4. It was red and _____ and blue.	gold salt
5. It _____ soft and warm.	golf felt
6. Rosa _____ it close.	bold held

Completing sentences with ending-blend words: lf, ld, lt

Basic Phonics Skills, Level C • EMC 3320 • ©2004 by Evan-Moor Corp.

Name _____

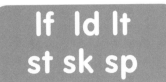
Look at each picture.
Read the sentences.
Copy the one that tells about the picture.

1.

The bird is in its nest.

My mask is funny.

_____

2.

My belt is big.

The gold is in the bag.

_____

3.

The pizza has a crust.

My desk is clean.

_____

4.

She likes her quilt.

The books are on the shelf.

_____

Review: Reading words with ending blends: sk, sp, st, lf, ld, lt

Ending Blends Review

lf ld lt st sk sp

Circle the word that best completes the sentence.

1. The _____ is under the _____.

west   **elf**   **quilt**

2. A _____ was on her _____.

wrist   **bald**   **wasp**

3. I played _____ in my _____.

vest   **elf**   **golf**

4. I put _____ on the _____.

roast   **salt**   **mask**

5. The _____ is in the stall.

gold   **golf**   **colt**

6. I hit my _____ with my _____.

desk   **wasp**   **fist**

7. I took the book off the _____.

salt   **shelf**   **quilt**

Review: Completing sentences with ending-blend words

Name _____

Blends at the End

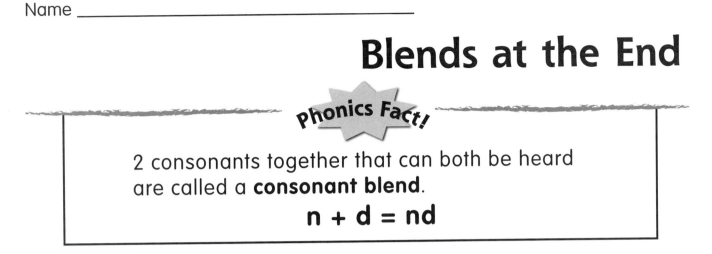

Phonics Fact!

2 consonants together that can both be heard
are called a **consonant blend**.

n + d = nd

Say the name of each picture.
Listen for the ending blend.
Draw a line to another picture that ends with that blend.
Write the sounds you hear on the lines.

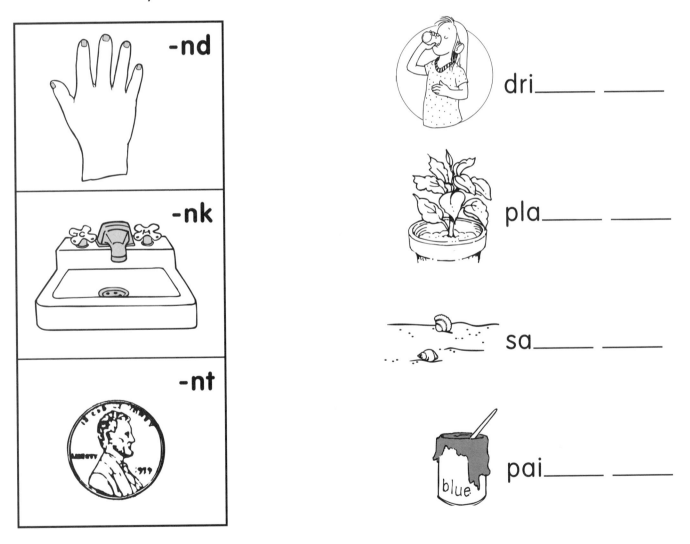

-nd

-nk

-nt

dri____ ____

pla____ ____

sa____ ____

pai____ ____

Distinguishing among ending blends: nd, nk, nt

Name _____

Consonant Blends

Fill in the circle by the sound you hear at
the end of each word.

1.   ○ nd
    ○ nk
    ○ nt

2.   ○ nd
    ○ nk
    ○ nt

3.   ○ nd
    ○ nk
    ○ nt

4.   ○ nd
    ○ nk
    ○ nt

5.   ○ nd
    ○ nk
    ○ nt

6.   ○ nd
    ○ nk
    ○ nt

7.   ○ nd
    ○ nk
    ○ nt

8.   ○ nd
    ○ nk
    ○ nt

Distinguishing among ending blends: nd, nk, nt

Basic Phonics Skills, Level C • EMC 3320 • ©2004 by Evan-Moor Corp.

Name _____

Name the picture.
Listen to the sounds.
Fill in the missing letters.

| -nd | -nk | -nt |

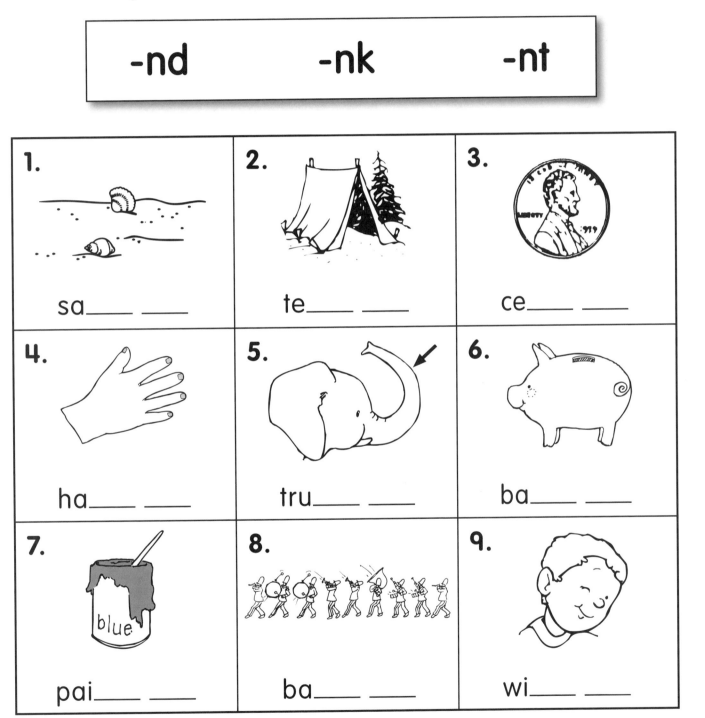

1.

sa____ ____

2.

te____ ____

3.

ce____ ____

4.

ha____ ____

5.

tru____ ____

6.

ba____ ____

7.

pai____ ____

8.

ba____ ____

9.

wi____ ____

Writing words with ending blends: nd, nk, nt

**Beginning & Ending 181
Consonant Blends**

Name _____

Write the Word

Say the word.
Write it on the line.

1.

_____

2.

_____

3.

_____

4.

_____

5.

_____

6.

blue

_____

7.

_____

8.

_____

9.

_____

Word Box

paint	trunk	drink	hand	bank
plant	sink	sand	cent	tank

Writing words with ending blends: **nd, nk, nt**

Basic Phonics Skills, Level C • EMC 3320 • ©2004 by Evan-Moor Corp.

Read Blends at the End

nd nk nt

Circle the word that best completes the sentence.

1. Nan and I _____ camping.

    went   **wand**   **wink**

2. We took a pink _____.

    thank   **tent**   **tend**

3. We _____ the day at the pond.

    spent   **send**   **sank**

4. The _____ blew hard.

    went   **wind**   **wink**

5. We sat on the river_____.

    bend   **bent**   **bank**

6. We played in the _____.

    sank   **sand**   **stunt**

7. I did not _____ it was fun.

    think   **plant**   **stand**

8. My friend did not _____ it.

    mink   **mint**   **mind**

Completing sentences with **nd, nk, nt** words

Beginning & Ending Consonant Blends

Blends at the End

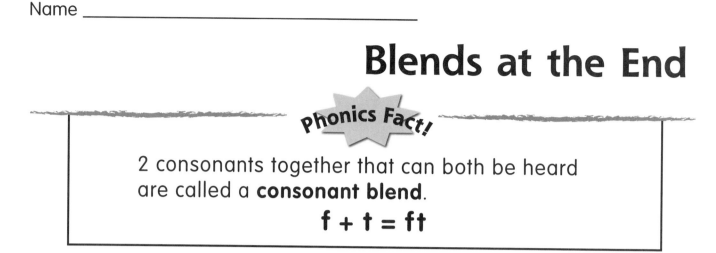

Phonics Fact!

2 consonants together that can both be heard
are called a **consonant blend**.

f + t = ft

Say the name of each picture.
Listen for the ending blend.
Draw a line to another picture that ends with that blend.
Write the sounds you hear on the lines.

-ft

-mp

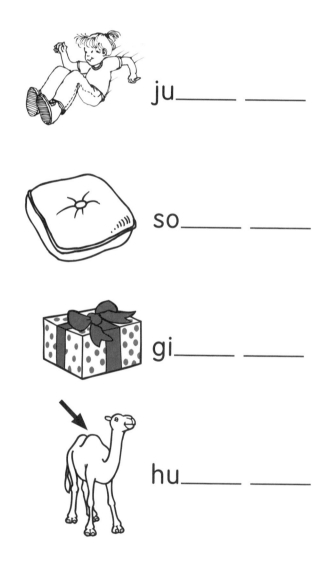

ju____ ____

so____ ____

gi____ ____

hu____ ____

Distinguishing between ending blends: ft, mp

Basic Phonics Skills, Level C • EMC 3320 • ©2004 by Evan-Moor Corp.

Name _____

Consonant Blends

Fill in the circle by the sound you hear at the end of each word.

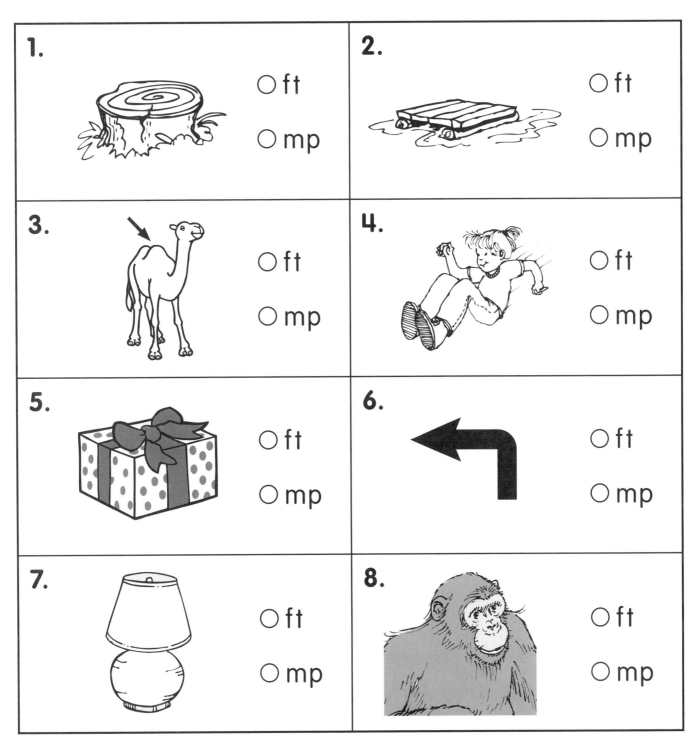

1.
○ ft
○ mp

2.
○ ft
○ mp

3.
○ ft
○ mp

4.
○ ft
○ mp

5.
○ ft
○ mp

6.
○ ft
○ mp

7.
○ ft
○ mp

8.
○ ft
○ mp

Distinguishing between ending blends: ft, mp

Name _____

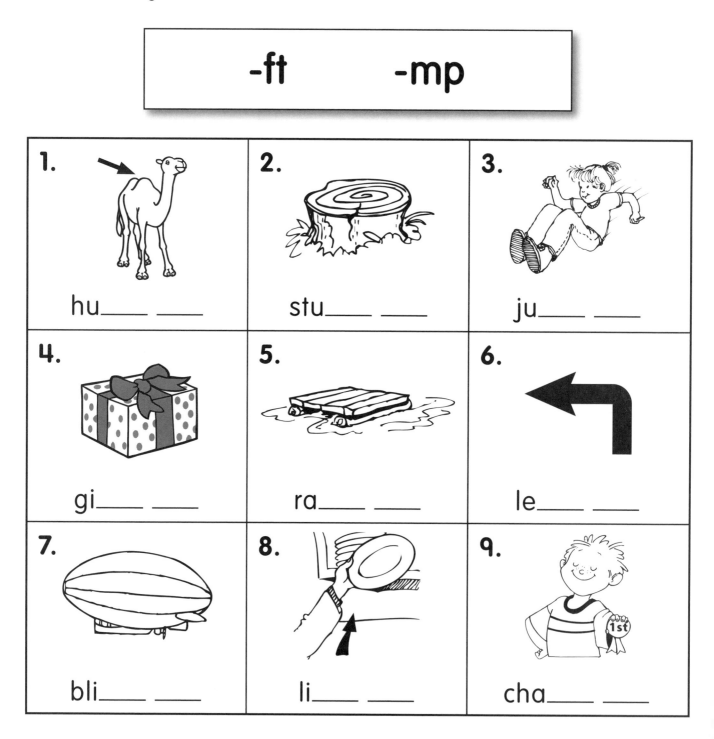

Listen for Ending Blends

Name the picture.
Listen to the sounds.
Fill in the missing letters.

-ft	-mp

1. hu____ ____

2. stu____ ____

3. ju____ ____

4. gi____ ____

5. ra____ ____

6. le____ ____

7. bli____ ____

8. li____ ____

9. cha____ ____

Writing words with ending blends: **ft, mp**

Basic Phonics Skills, Level C • EMC 3320 • ©2004 by Evan-Moor Corp.

Name _____

Circle the word that best completes
the sentence.

1. Lin went to give the king a _____.
    gift   **bump**   **lift**

2. She rode on a _____ down the river.
    gift   **camp**   **raft**

3. She had to _____ by the river.
    lamp   **camp**   **raft**

4. She sat on a _____ to rest.
    stick   **sift**   **stump**

5. She walked up a _____ to the castle.
    stump   **ramp**   **lift**

6. Lin's gift to the king was a _____.
    lamp   **left**   **damp**

7. The king liked his _____ very much.
    lift   **shift**   **gift**

8. Then Lin _____ to go home.
    left   **skimp**   **lump**

Completing sentences with ending-blend words

Name _____

Let's Go Fishing

Choose a word from the word box to fill in each blank.

1. Ben woke up early. He turned on the _____

and _____ out of bed.

2. Today, he and Dad were going to

their fishing _____.

3. It was still dark when they _____ home.

4. They pulled the _____ down the

_____ to the water.

5. The camp was on the other side of the _____.

6. "The water is not _____," said Dad.

7. "Let's _____ a bit. Maybe we can catch
some fish."

Word Box				
left	raft	camp	jumped	lamp
swift	drift	swamp	ramp	

Completing sentences with ending-blend words

Basic Phonics Skills, Level C • EMC 3320 • ©2004 by Evan-Moor Corp.

Name _____

Circle the word that names the picture.

1.		stomp	stump	stamp
2.		raft	lamp	stamp
3.		trap	hand	lamp
4.		mask	trunk	dunk
5.		tent	gift	soft
6.		blind	hand	find
7.		plant	print	paint
8.		gift	lift	tent

Review: Reading words with ending blends: nd, nk, nt, ft, mp

Beginning & Ending 189
Consonant Blends

Blends Everywhere!

Choose the correct word to complete each sentence.

1. Sam _____ most of his money on food at the fair.

2. Red Hen will _____ the wheat to make flour.

3. "I will _____ you three wishes," said the elf.

4. The tire went "_____" when it went flat.

5. The river is too _____ to swim across.

6. Did you smell that _____?

7. We like to _____ our feet in time with the tune.

8. Did you _____ the cookie in your milk?

Word Box				
spent	stomp	grind	skunk	swift
grant	blink	stand	thump	dunk

Review: Completing sentences with **nd, nk, nt, ft, mp** words

Name _____

Ending Blends Review

Look at each picture.
Read the sentences.
Copy the one that tells about the picture.

1.

The wasp buzzed on.
I like your mask.

_____

2.

Turn off the lamp.
Don't fall off the raft.

_____

3.

The bird is in the nest.
The book fell off the shelf.

_____

Circle the words in the sentences above with these ending blends.
Can you find one word for each blend?
Cross out the ones you can <u>not</u> find.

-st	-sk	-sp	-lf	-ld	-lt
-nd	-nk	-nt	-ft	-mp	-ng

Review: Reading words with ending consonant blends

Review
Blends at the End
lf ld lt nd nk nt

Choose the correct word to complete each sentence.

1. The _____ pushed the sailboat across the lake.

2. A penny is the same as one _____.

3. The little _____ ate hay in the barn.

4. Fill the _____ with water to wash the dishes.

5. The chips are nice and _____.

6. The blue book goes on the top _____.

7. Will you _____ my _____ as we cross the road?

8. I got the _____ _____ in the store. There are no more _____.

Word Box					
hold	cent	shelf	sink	mask	colt
crisp	last	wind	hand	left	

Review: Completing sentences with lf, ld, lt, nd, nk, nt words

Plural and Inflectional Endings

Name _____

More Than One

Look at the picture.
Circle the correct word.

boy

boys

1.  cup cups	**2.**  cup cups
3. 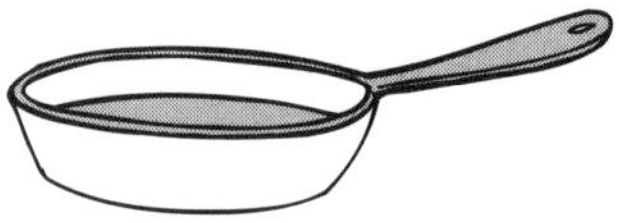 pan pans	**4.**  pan pans
5.  can cans	**6.**  can cans
7.  top tops	**8.** 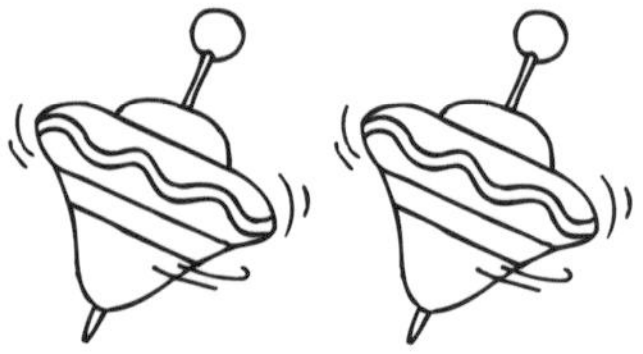 top tops

Distinguishing between singular and plural forms

Name _____

Phonics Fact!

If there is more than one, you add **es** after **s**, **sh**, **ch**, or **x**.

Write the word to say more than one.

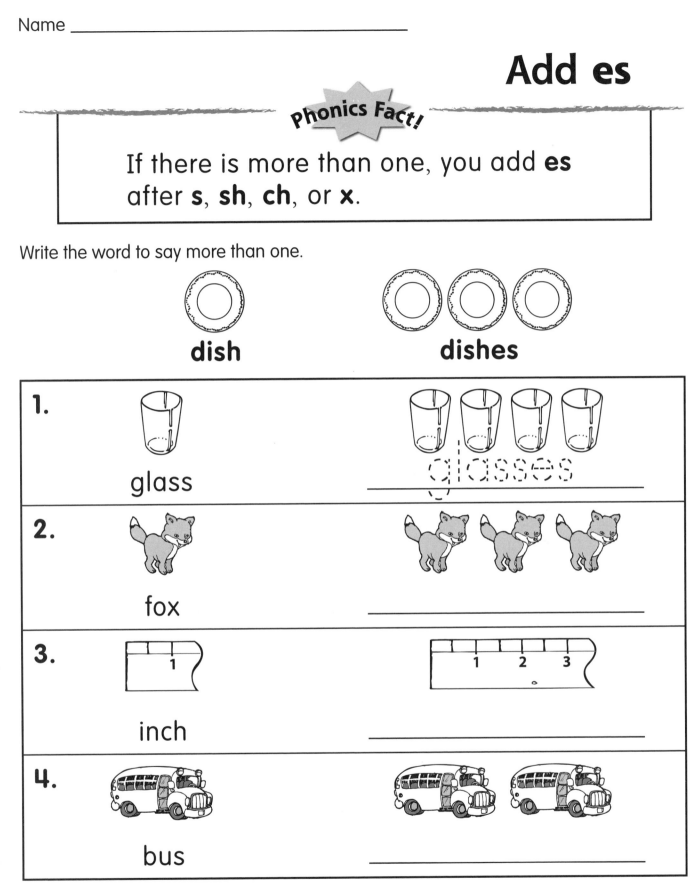

dish   **dishes**

1.	glass	ḡḹãśśẽś
2.	fox	_____
3.	inch	_____
4.	bus	_____

On the back of this page, write a sentence using the word **foxes**.

Adding es to form plurals

What Do You Add?

Write the words in the correct box.

hats

Add **s** to say
more than one.

_____

_____

_____

dresses

Add **es** after **s**, **sh**,
ch, or **x**.

_____

_____

_____

Word Box

dish	plate	box	car
bed	inch	wish	pig

Use the words above to fill in the blanks.

1. I need five _____ of ribbon.

2. How many dirty _____ did he wash?

Adding **s** or **es** to form plurals

Watch for y

Phonics Fact!

If there is more than one and the word ends in **y**, change the **y** to **i** and add **es**.

pon**y**   pon**ies**

Write the word that says more than one.

More Than One

1.	bunny	_____
2.	cherry	_____
3.	fairy	_____

Write a word from above in each blank.

1. I ate 5 _____.

2. The 2 _____ hopped away.

3. There were 3 _____ in the story.

Writing plural forms of words ending in y

Name _____

Make a Choice

Write the words in the correct box. Make them plural.

hat<u>s</u> **s** (says more than **1**)	**dish<u>es</u>** **es** (if a word ends in **s**, **sh**, **ch**, or **x**)	**pon<u>ies</u>** **ies** (drop **y** and add **ies**)
_____ _____ _____	_____ _____ _____	_____ _____ _____

Word Box

cup	baby	box
lady	egg	hen
inch	wish	bunny

Use the words above to fill in the blanks.

1. The hen laid six _____ .

2. Put the 2 empty _____ in the car.

3. I know all _____ love carrots.

Review: Plural forms with s, es, ies

Name _____

More Than One

Circle the correct word in each row that means more than one.

1. chair	chares	(chairs)	charies
2. pan	panes	panies	pans
3. dish	dishs	dishes	dishies
4. lady	ladys	ladyes	ladies
5. dress	dresss	dresses	dressies
6. inch	inches	inchs	inchies
7. fox	foxs	foxes	foxies
8. clock	clockies	clockes	clocks

Review: Plural forms with s, es, ies

Name _____

Add Endings

s, ed, or ing

Circle the word that best completes the sentence.

1. The frog was _____ off the log.

    jumps   **jumped**   **jumping**

2. Carlos _____ ball last year.

    plays   **played**   **playing**

3. Now she _____ rope all the time.

    jumps   **jumped**   **jumping**

4. He is _____ on the corner.

    waits   **waited**   **waiting**

5. Lee _____ to go yesterday.

    wants   **wanted**   **wanting**

6. If she _____ up, she will see a rainbow.

    looks   **looked**   **looking**

7. The puppy is _____ his paw.

    licks   **licked**   **licking**

8. Sally _____ her mom yesterday.

    calls   **called**   **calling**

Choosing words with the correct inflectional ending: -s, -ed, -ing

Name _____

Endings

-s -ing -ed

Choose the correct ending.
Write the word on the line.

1. She _____ to school last week.

    walks   **walked**   **walking**

2. Kim _____ to come with us now.

    wants   **wanted**   **wanting**

3. Lee is _____ on a farm.

    works   **worked**   **working**

4. Tom is _____ all kinds of fruit.

    picks   **picked**   **picking**

5. Carmen _____ the page.

    turns   **turned**   **turning**

6. Joe is _____ a red wagon.

    pulls   **pulled**   **pulling**

7. Jake _____ over the stream.

    jumps   **jumped**   **jumping**

8. Tanya _____ with her sister yesterday.

    plays   **played**   **playing**

Choosing words with the correct inflectional ending: **-s, -ed, -ing**

Name _____

Silent e

Drop the silent **e**, and then add the ending.

| wav**e** | wav**ed** | wav**ing** |

X out **e**	Add **ed**	Add **ing**
slice		
poke		
like		
tape		
hike		

Choose words from above to fill in the blanks.

1. The boy _____ up the trail.

2. She _____ the box shut.

3. I am _____ the bread.

Adding ed and ing to words ending with silent e

Syllabication

BASIC Phonics Skills

Name _____

I Can Count Syllables

Say the name of the picture.
Count the syllables.
Circle the number you hear.

1. 1 ②2 3

2. 1 2 3

3. 1 2 3

4. 1 2 3

5. 1 2 3

6. 1 2 3

7. 1 2 3

8. 1 2 3

9. 1 2 3

Counting 1-, 2-, and 3-syllable words

Basic Phonics Skills, Level C • EMC 3320 • ©2004 by Evan-Moor Corp.

Name _____

Color:

1 syllable	2 syllables	3 syllables
yellow	blue	green

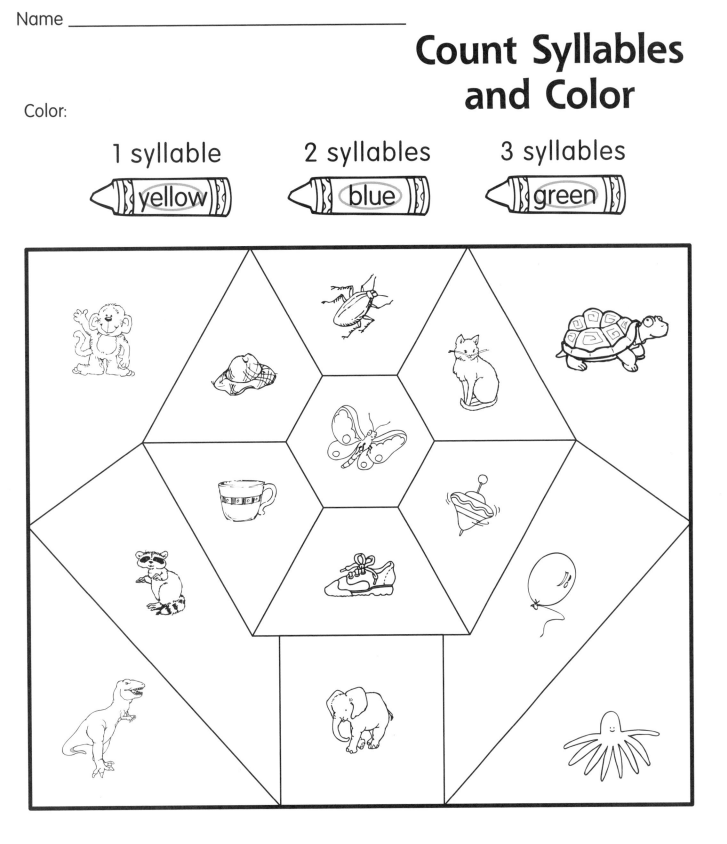

I see a _____. **airplane flower dog**

Counting 1-, 2-, and 3-syllable words

Name _____

Cut and Paste Syllables

Cut out the words. Count the syllables.
Paste them in the correct boxes.

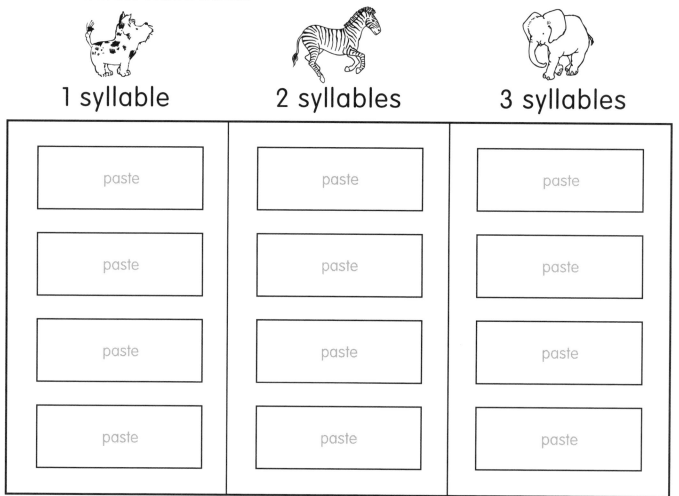

1 syllable | 2 syllables | 3 syllables

paste	paste	paste
paste	paste	paste
paste	paste	paste
paste	paste	paste

baby	hand	truck	away
butterfly	telephone	block	family
sister	funny	Saturday	box

Sorting 1-, 2-, and 3-syllable words

Basic Phonics Skills, Level C • EMC 3320 • ©2004 by Evan-Moor Corp.

Name _____

2-Syllable Hunt

Color the 2-syllable words red to
help Mouse get to the cheese.

bunny	nibble	red	hill
goat	cupcake	puppy	ball
fast	seed	yellow	happy
ten	sun	snake	sunny

Choose 2-syllable words from above to fill in the blanks.

1. The mouse saw some _____ cheese.

2. He was so _____.

3. He loves to _____ on cheese.

Identifying 2-syllable words

©2004 by Evan-Moor Corp. • Basic Phonics Skills, Level C • EMC 3320

Name _____

3-Syllable Search

Color the 3-syllable words green to help
Dinosaur get to his cave.

dinosaur	butterfly	pancake	five
after	grandmother	swing	silly
family	pajamas	better	bubble
Saturday	hill	orange	pink
wonderful	telephone	everything	octopus

Choose 3-syllable words from above to fill in the blanks.

1. Dino was a busy _____.

2. He had been to visit his _____.

3. He was going home on _____.

Identifying 3-syllable words

Basic Phonics Skills, Level C • EMC 3320 • ©2004 by Evan-Moor Corp.

Word Families

How to Make Word Family Sliders

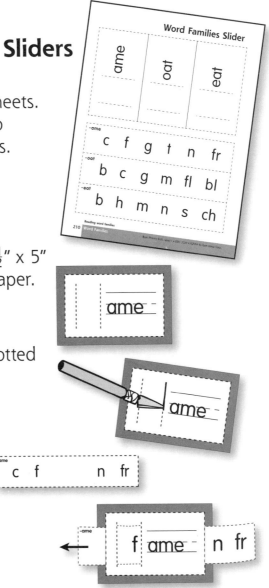

1. Reproduce the word family slider sheets. Select the word families you wish to practice, and cut on the dotted lines.

2. Glue the word family holder to a $3\frac{1}{2}$" x 5" (9 x 13 cm) piece of construction paper.

3. Use a craft knife to slit along the dotted lines on the word family holders.

4. Insert the correct letter strip.

5. Demonstrate to students how to pull the strip through the holder.

Word Families Slider

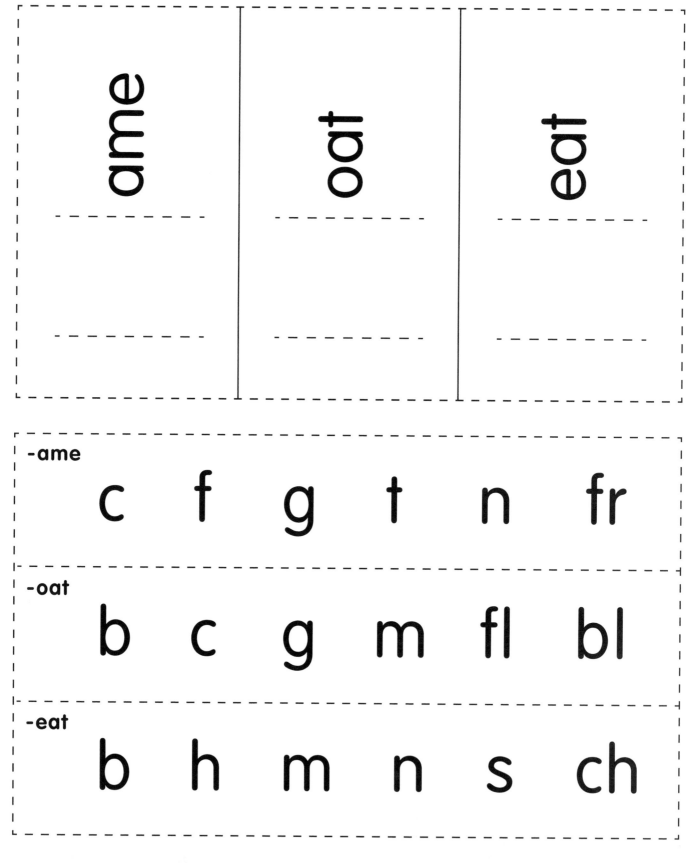

ame

oat

eat

-ame

c f g t n fr

-oat

b c g m fl bl

-eat

b h m n s ch

Reading word families

Basic Phonics Skills, Level C • EMC 3320 • ©2004 by Evan-Moor Corp.

Look Carefully

-ame -oat -eat

Circle the word that names the picture.

1.		fame	name	game
2.		coat	boat	goat
3.		seat	heat	beat
4.		flame	frame	tame
5.	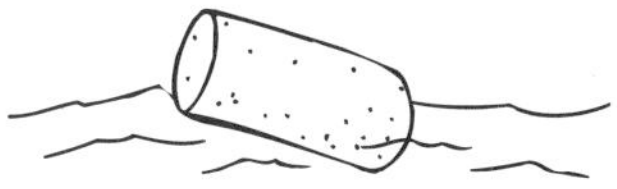	boat	bloat	float
6.	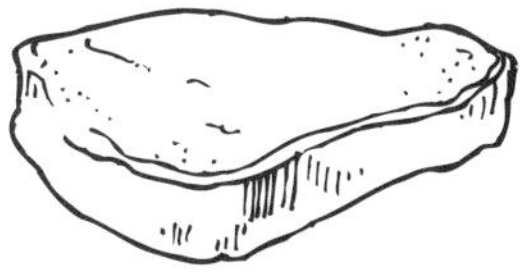	neat	meat	seat
7.		fame	tame	frame
8.		coat	boat	float

Reading word families

Name _____

Make New Words

Write a letter or letters on each line to make a new word.

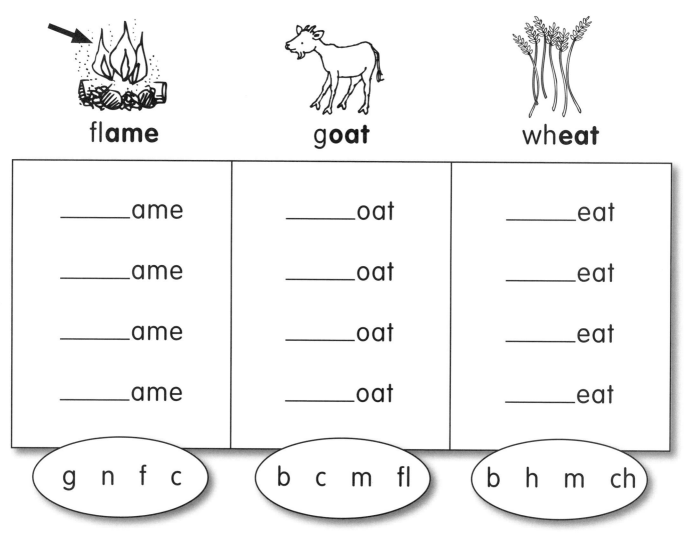

flame   **goat**   **wheat**

_____ame	_____oat	_____eat
_____ame	_____oat	_____eat
_____ame	_____oat	_____eat
_____ame	_____oat	_____eat

g n f c   b c m fl   b h m ch

Fill in each blank with a word from above.

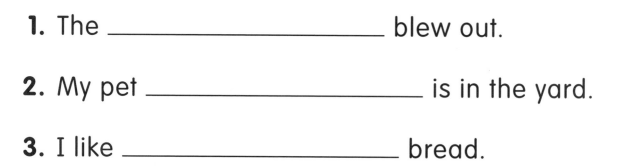

1. The _____ blew out.

2. My pet _____ is in the yard.

3. I like _____ bread.

Puzzle Time

Color the word families to solve the puzzle.

-ame
gray

-oat
red

-eat
blue

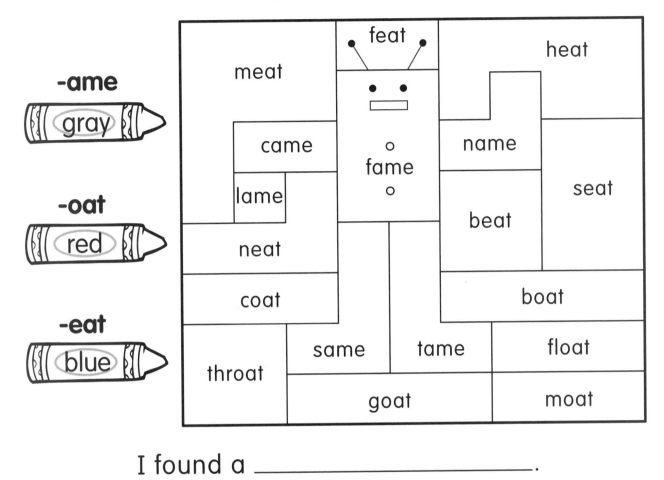

I found a _____.

Copy the words from the puzzle in the correct box.

-ame	-oat	-eat
came		

Name _____

Read Word Families

-ame
-oat
-eat

Circle the word that best completes the sentence.

1. I _____ to school late.

      fame   **came**   **tame**

2. Please take a _____.

      seat   **meat**   **heat**

3. We call the _____ Gus.

      boat   **coat**   **goat**

4. I like to play that _____.

      came   **game**   **name**

5. Put on your _____ when it's cold.

      coat   **goat**   **moat**

6. I like to _____ the drum.

      seat   **heat**   **beat**

Choosing the correct word-family words to complete sentences

Word Families

-ame -oat -eat

Choose the correct words from each
word family to fill in the blanks.

1. I _____ home after the _____.

name	game	came

2. My _____ is ready to _____.

float	goat	boat

3. Is it a _____ to eat _____?

meat	treat	beat

Write 2 words for each word family.

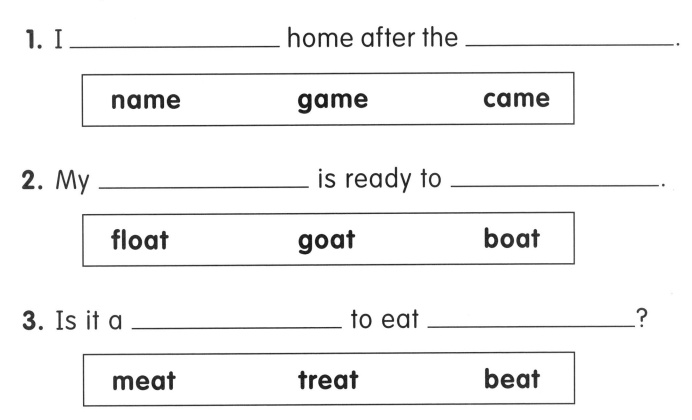

-oat	**-ame**	**-eat**
_____	_____	_____
_____	_____	_____

Choosing the correct word-family words to complete sentences

The Goat

-ame -oat -eat

Use the words in the word box to
complete the sentences.

1. I have a pet _____ named

Billy. He is not wild. He is _____.

2. I like to play _____ with him.

3. When he wants to _____, he will

_____ until I feed him.

4. He likes _____ the best.

5. I think he is a _____ pet.

Word Box

neat	games	tame	eat
goat	bleat	oats	

Choosing the correct word-family words to complete sentences

Word Families Slider

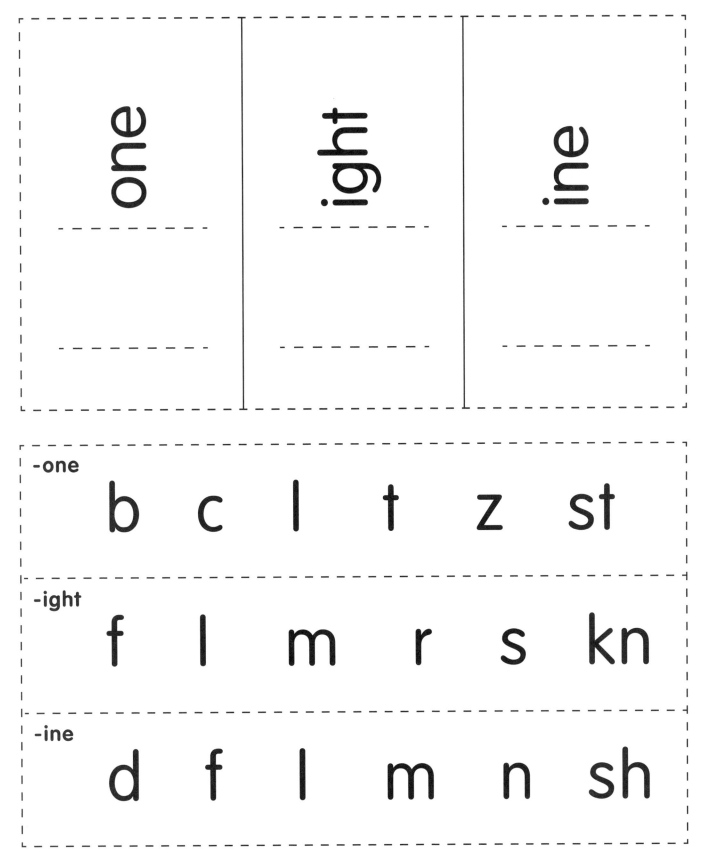

one

ight

ine

-one

b c l t z st

-ight

f l m r s kn

-ine

d f l m n sh

Reading word families

Look Carefully
-one -ight -ine

Circle the word that names the picture.

1.		bone	lone	cone
2.		fight	light	sight
3.		line	fine	nine
4.		cone	bone	stone
5.		light	night	right
6.		fine	mine	nine
7.		stone	alone	bone
8.		night	sight	right

Reading word families

 Basic Phonics Skills, Level C • EMC 3320 • ©2004 by Evan-Moor Corp.

Name 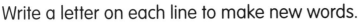 _____

Make New Words

Write a letter on each line to make new words.

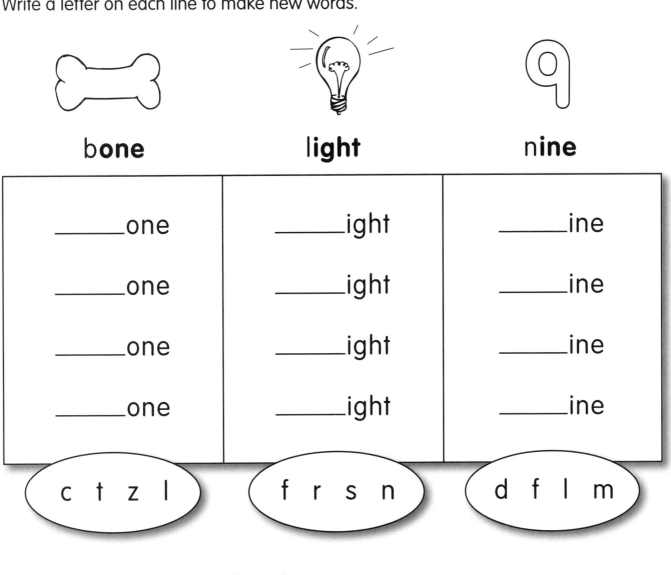

bone   **l**ight   **n**ine

____one	____ight	____ine
____one	____ight	____ine
____one	____ight	____ine
____one	____ight	____ine

c t z l   f r s n   d f l m

Fill in each blank with a word from above.

1. My dog hid his _____ .

2. Turn on the _____ .

3. Soon I will be _____ years old.

Writing word families

Name _____

Puzzle Time

Color the word families to solve the puzzle.

-ine
yellow

-ight
brown

-one
red

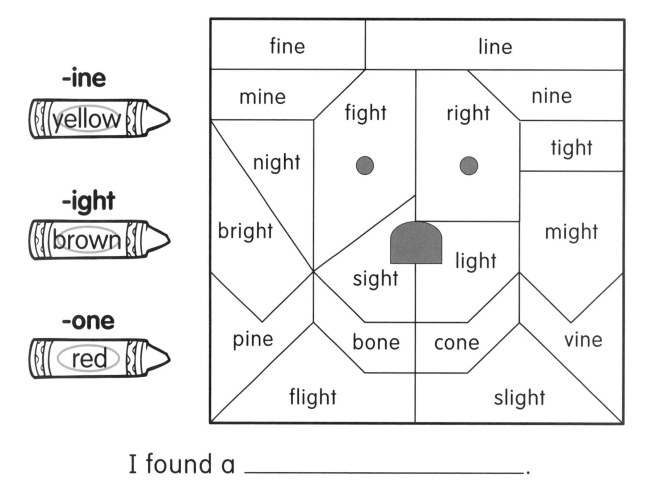

I found a _____.

Copy the words from the puzzle in the correct box.

-ine	**-ight**	**-one**
nine		

Writing word families

Basic Phonics Skills, Level C • EMC 3320 • ©2004 by Evan-Moor Corp.

Name _____

Read Word Families

Circle the word that best completes the sentence.

1. That is a No Parking _____.

      tone   **zone**   **bone**

2. The _____ is dim.

      right   **sight**   **light**

3. You did a _____ job today.

      fine   **mine**   **shine**

4. The bell had a nice _____ when it rang.

      cone   **bone**   **tone**

5. I _____ go on a trip soon.

      sight   **light**   **might**

6. There are _____ of us at home.

      nine   **dine**   **fine**

Choosing the correct word-family words to complete sentences

Name _____

The Dragon and the Knight

-one -ight -ine

Use the words in the word box to complete the sentences.

1. The dragon lives _____ in a cave.

2. He is nice. He doesn't like to _____.

3. In fact, he is a friend to a _____.

4. They _____ together each day.

5. The knight eats the meat. The dragon chews on

   the _____.

6. They are a funny _____ together.

Word Box		
fight	alone	dine
bone	knight	sight

Choosing the correct word-family words to complete sentences

Basic Phonics Skills, Level C • EMC 3320 • ©2004 by Evan-Moor Corp.

Name _____

Word Families

-one -ight -ine

Choose the correct word from each
word family to fill in the blanks.

1. Does the dog want a _____?

tone	bone	lone

2. We need a light when it is _____.

night	sight	fight

3. There is a long line waiting to _____.

fine	dine	mine

Write 2 words for each word family.

-one	-ight	-ine
_____	_____	_____
_____	_____	_____

Choosing the correct word-family words to complete sentences

Word Families Slider

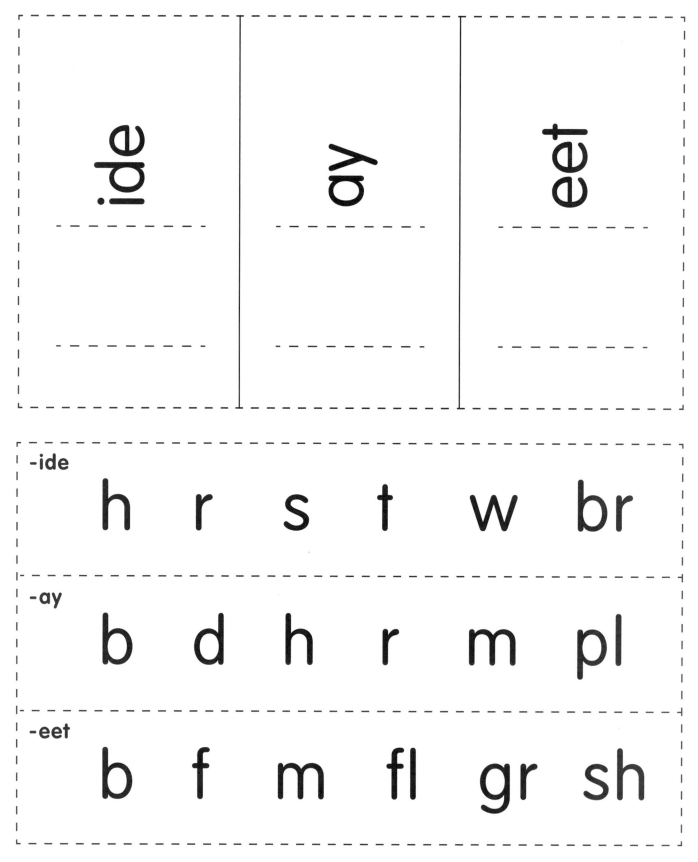

ide

ay

eet

-ide

h r s t w br

-ay

b d h r m pl

-eet

b f m fl gr sh

Reading word families

Basic Phonics Skills, Level C • EMC 3320 • ©2004 by Evan-Moor Corp.

Look Carefully
-ide -ay -eet

Circle the word that names the picture.

1. 		say	hay	lay
2. 		ride	hide	bride
3. 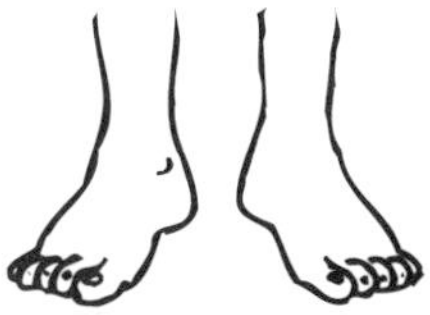		feet	meet	sweet
4. 		hide	slide	wide
5. 		say	way	gray
6. 		feet	meet	beet
7. 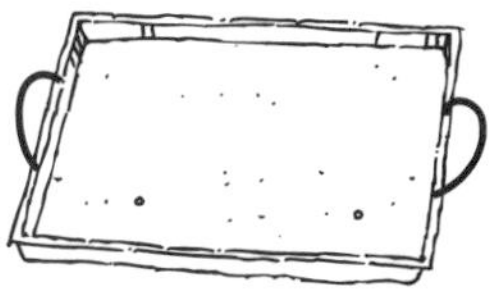		stay	tray	way
8. 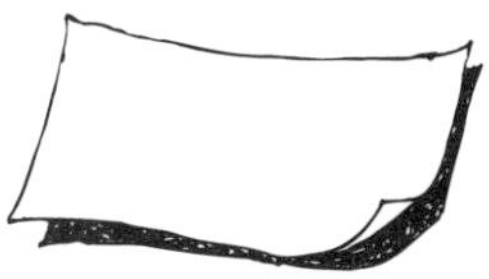		sheet	beet	meet

Reading word families

Name _____

Make New Words

Write a letter or letters on each line to make a new word.

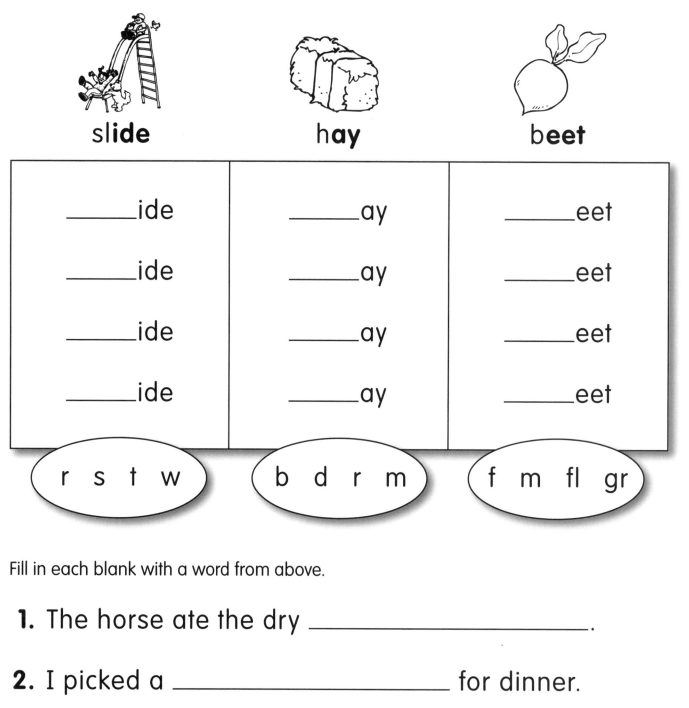

sl**ide**   h**ay**   b**eet**

____ide	____ay	____eet
____ide	____ay	____eet
____ide	____ay	____eet
____ide	____ay	____eet

r s t w   b d r m   f m fl gr

Fill in each blank with a word from above.

1. The horse ate the dry _____.

2. I picked a _____ for dinner.

3. I will zoom down the _____.

Name _____

Puzzle Time

Color the word families to solve the puzzle.

-ide
red

-eet
green

-ay
blue

-ame
yellow

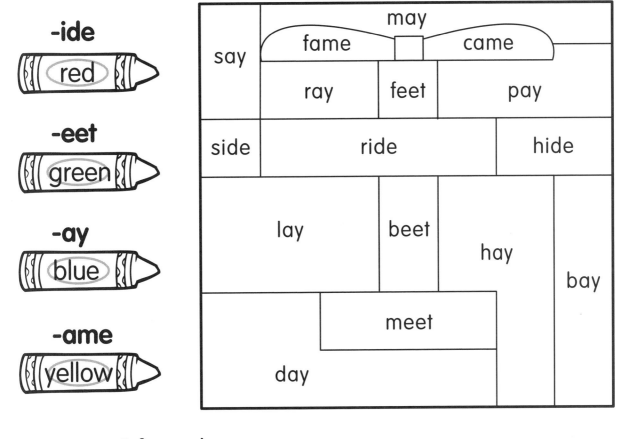

I found a _____.

Copy the words from the puzzle in the correct box.

-ay	-ame	-eet	-ide
ray			

Writing word families

©2004 by Evan-Moor Corp. • Basic Phonics Skills, Level C • EMC 3320

Word Families 227

Name _____

-ide
-ay
-eet

Circle the word that best completes the sentence.

1. Lay the box on its _____.

    tide   **wide**   **side**

2. The _____ is sunny.

    day   **may**   **hay**

3. Can we _____ today?

    beet   **feet**   **meet**

4. A six-lane road is _____.

    hide   **wide**   **side**

5. _____ I have a cookie?

    Hay   **Say**   **May**

6. My _____ are size 4.

    meet   **feet**   **beet**

Choosing the correct word-family words to complete sentences

Name _____

Word Families
-ide -ay -eet

Choose the correct words from each
word family to fill in the blanks.

1. I will _____ on the _____ path.

wide	ride	tide

2. I _____ sing to you to_____.

may	ray	day

3. We will _____ on the _____.

beet	meet	street

Write 2 words for each word family.

-ide	-ay	-eet
_____	_____	_____
_____	_____	_____

Choosing the correct word-family words to complete sentences

Name _____

The Pirates

-ide -ay -eet

Use the words in the word box to complete the sentences.

1. Can you come over _____?

2. We can _____ and be pirates.

3. A box will be our boat. We can use a _____ as a sail.

4. We will fight side by _____.

5. My mom will _____ play gold for us to find. Then we can count it.

Word Box		
play	hide	sheet
side	today	

Choosing the correct word-family words to complete sentences

Basic Phonics Skills, Level C • EMC 3320 • ©2004 by Evan-Moor Corp.

Word Families Slider

eak

old

eed

-eak

b   l   p   w   sp   str

-old

b   c   f   g   h   t

-eed

d   f   n   s   w   bl

Reading word families

Look Carefully
-eak -old -eed

Circle the word that names the picture.

1.		leak	weak	beak
2.		told	fold	sold
3.		deed	seed	feed
4.		hold	told	gold
5.		weed	need	seed
6.		leak	peak	beak
7.		seed	need	feed
8.		told	sold	hold

Reading word families

Name _____

Make New Words

Write a letter or letters on each line to make new words.

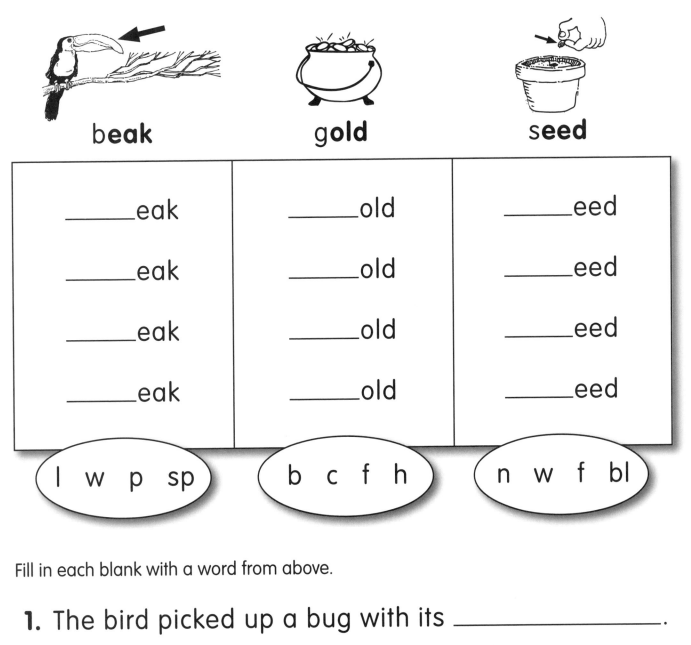

b**eak**   g**old**   s**eed**

_____eak	_____old	_____eed
_____eak	_____old	_____eed
_____eak	_____old	_____eed
_____eak	_____old	_____eed

l w p sp   b c f h   n w f bl

Fill in each blank with a word from above.

1. The bird picked up a bug with its _____.

2. I put all the _____ in the bank.

3. You should plant your _____ in April.

Writing word families

©2004 by Evan-Moor Corp. • Basic Phonics Skills, Level C • EMC 3320

Word Families 233

Puzzle Time

Color the word families to solve the puzzle.

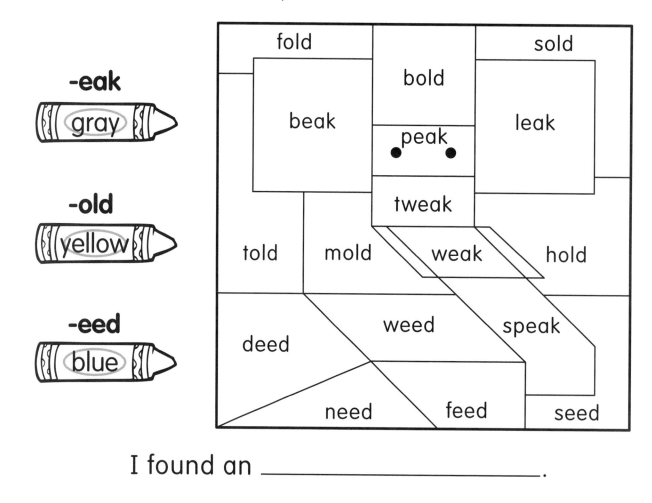

-eak
gray

-old
yellow

-eed
blue

fold   sold
bold
beak   peak   leak
tweak
told   mold   weak   hold
weed   speak
deed
need   feed   seed

I found an _____.

Copy the words from the puzzle in the correct box.

-eak	-old	-eed

Read Word Families

-eak
-old
-eed

Circle the word that best completes the sentence.

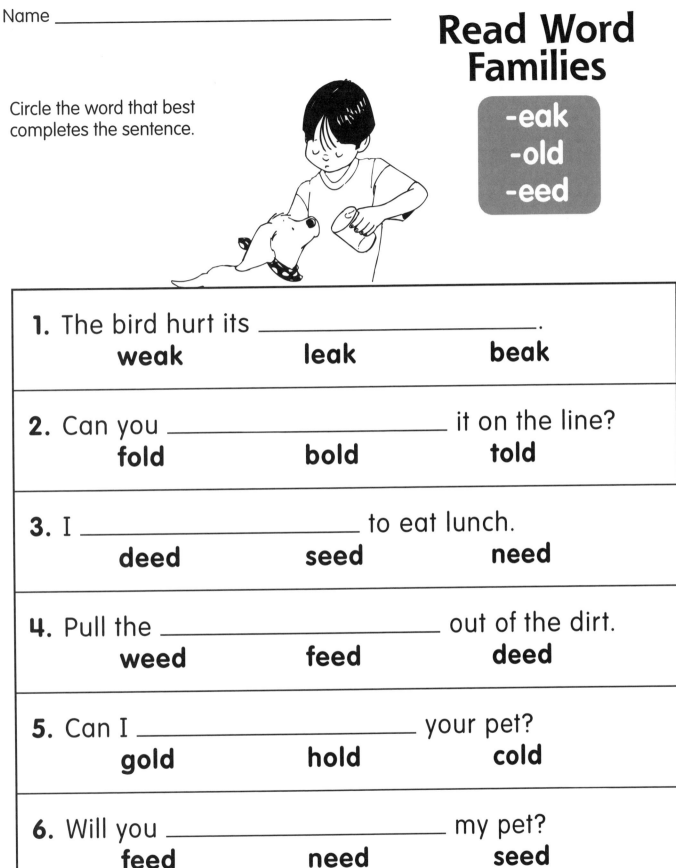

1. The bird hurt its _____.

     weak   **leak**   **beak**

2. Can you _____ it on the line?

     fold   **bold**   **told**

3. I _____ to eat lunch.

     deed   **seed**   **need**

4. Pull the _____ out of the dirt.

     weed   **feed**   **deed**

5. Can I _____ your pet?

     gold   **hold**   **cold**

6. Will you _____ my pet?

     feed   **need**   **seed**

Choosing the correct word-family words to complete sentences

Name _____

Word Families
-eak -old -eed

Choose the correct words from each word family to fill in the blanks.

1. Please _____ up if you see a _____ in the sink.

peak	speak	leak

2. I was _____ it is a _____ ring.

gold	told	cold

3. We _____ to _____ the cats.

feed	need	seed

Write 2 words for each word family.

-eak	-old	-eed
_____	_____	_____
_____	_____	_____

Choosing the correct word-family words to complete sentences

Basic Phonics Skills, Level C • EMC 3320 • ©2004 by Evan-Moor Corp.

Name _____

The Big Seed

Use the words in the word box to
complete the sentences.

1. The blue bird needs to _____.

2. He saw a big _____.

3. He took the seed in his _____.

4. He could not _____ the seed.

5. It fell into the _____.

6. The blue bird _____ to find a small seed.

Word Box		
seed	beak	needs
hold	eat	weeds

Choosing the correct word-family words to complete sentences

Little Phonics Readers

Long Vowel Readers

Word Family Readers

How to Reproduce the Little Phonics Readers

1. Reproduce the Little Phonics Readers and cut on the dotted line.

2. Fold both sheets as indicated.

3. Stack the pages as shown.

4. Staple inside.

238

Make a Cake

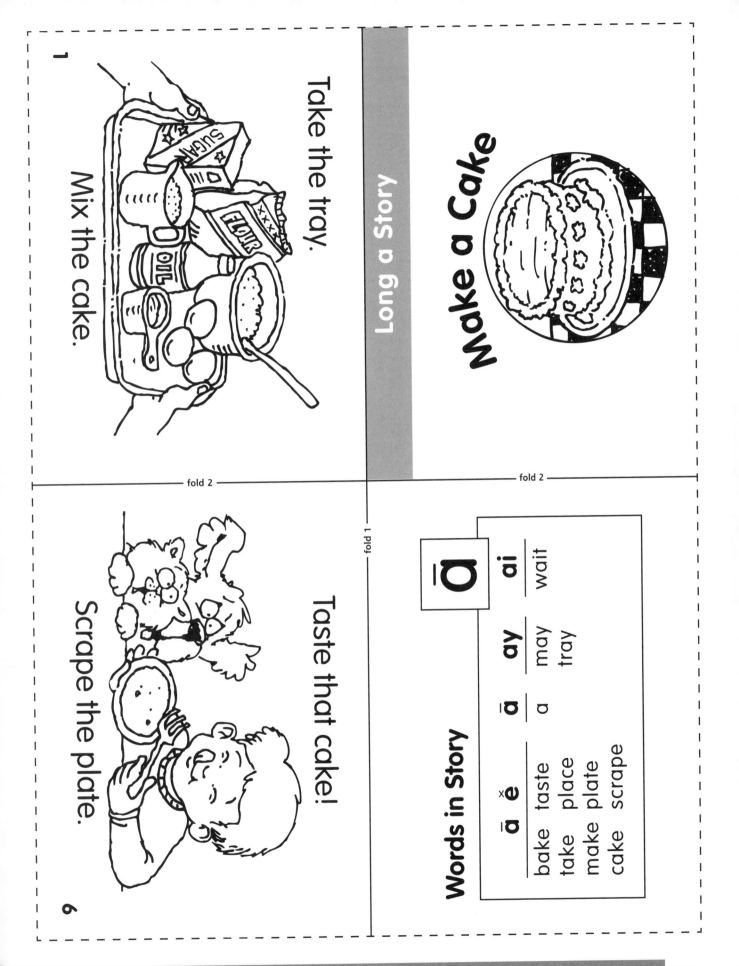

1

Take the tray.

Mix the cake.

6

Taste that cake!

Scrape the plate.

Words in Story

ā e	ā	ay	ai
	a	may	wait
		tray	

bake taste
take place
make plate
cake scrape

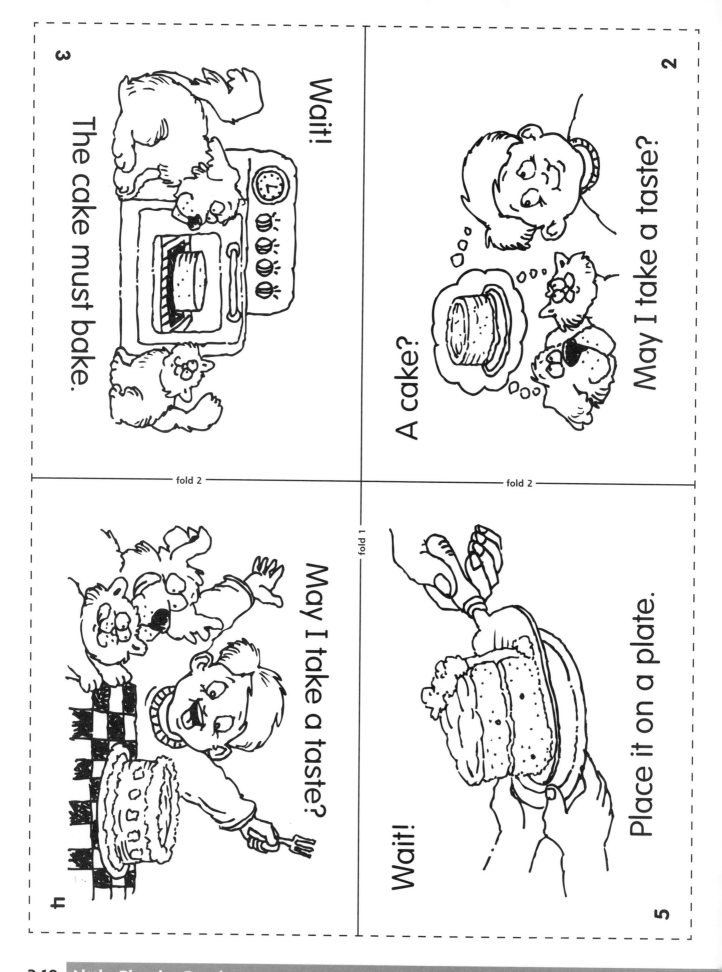

3

Wait!

The cake must bake.

2

May I take a taste?

A cake?

4

May I take a taste?

5

Wait!

Place it on a plate.

fold 2

fold 2

fold 1

Basic Phonics Skills, Level C • EMC 3320 • ©2004 by Evan-Moor Corp.

1

Lee needs seeds.

Lee's Seeds

See Lee's peas and beets.

We will eat them.

6

Words in Story

$\bar{e}$

$\bar{e}$ $\overset{x}{e}$	$\bar{e}$ $\bar{e}$	ee	ea
these	he	Lee	pea
	we	seeds	leaves
		needs	eat
		beet	
		see	

3

He plants the beet seeds.

2

He plants the pea seeds.

fold 2

fold 2

fold 1

The seeds need these:

See the leaves.

4

5

1

Try it on.
Pick the right size.
Tie it tight.

My Bike

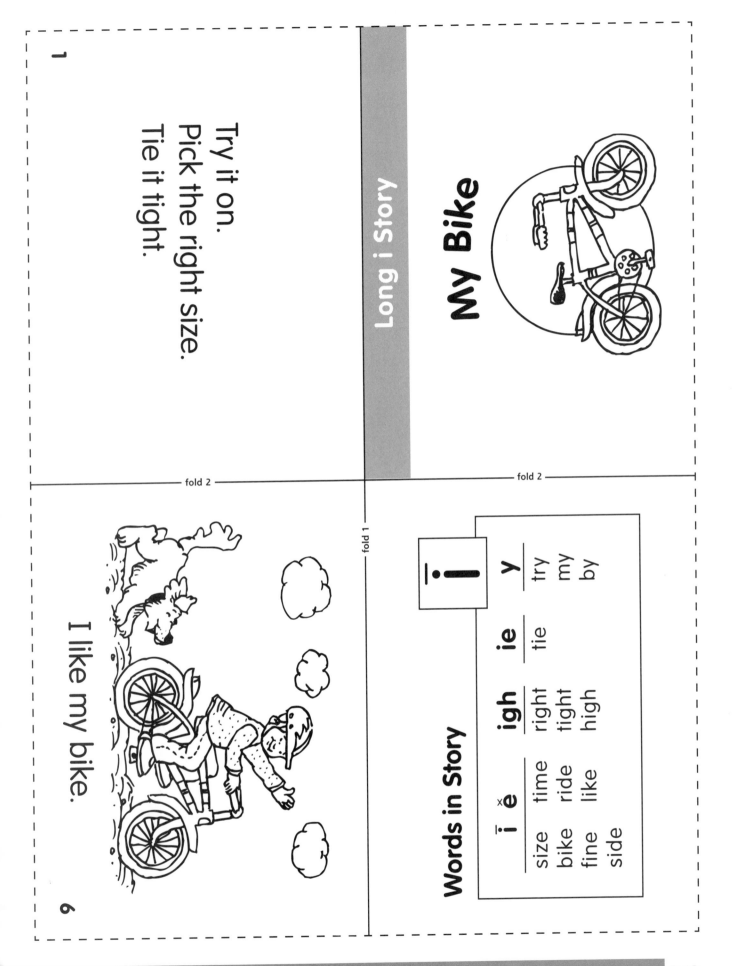

I like my bike.

6

Words in Story

ī	i̵e	igh	ie	y
size	time	right	tie	try
bike	ride	tight		my
fine	like	high		by
side				

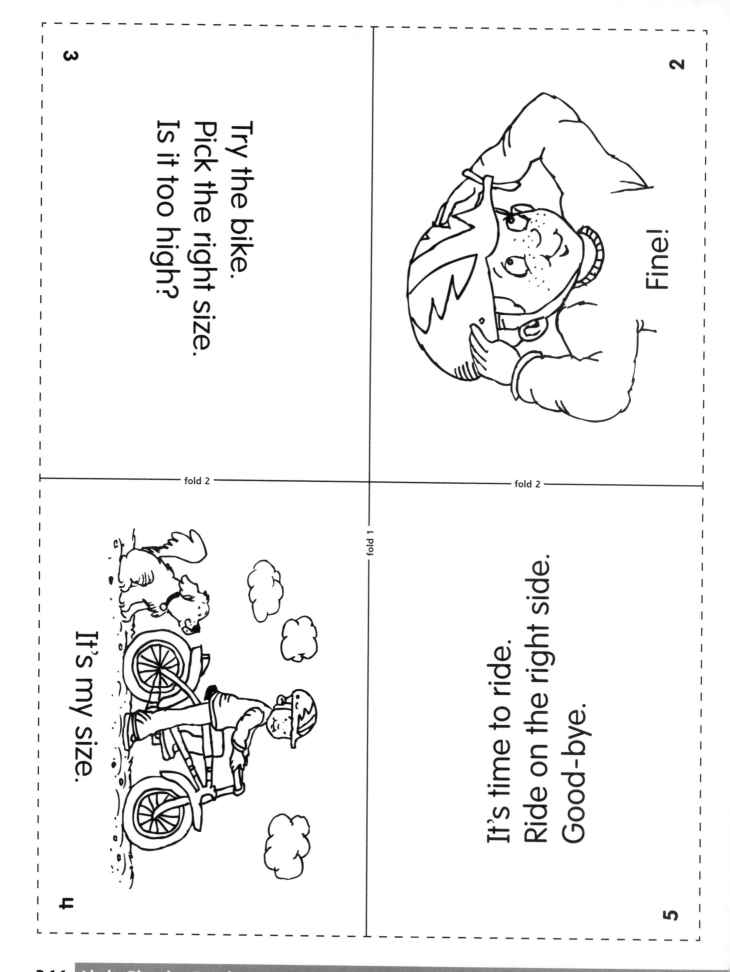

3

Try the bike.
Pick the right size.
Is it too high?

2

Fine!

fold 2 — fold 2

fold 1

4

It's my size.

5

It's time to ride.
Ride on the right side.
Good-bye.

Basic Phonics Skills, Level C • EMC 3320 • ©2004 by Evan-Moor Corp.

1

Close the hole!

Long o Story

Joan & the Coach

Joan drove it home.

fold 2

fold 1

fold 2

Words in Story

ō̄e	ō̄	oa	ow
	go	Joan	low
		coach	
		goal	

ō̄ e
close score
hole drove
dove home
stole

9

Basic Phonics Skills, Level C • EMC 3320 • ©2004 by Evan-Moor Corp.

1

A Cute Mule

fold 2

fold 2

fold 1

9

A cute mule
in a blue uniform
makes music on a ukulele.

Words in Story

ū×e	ū	ui	ue
mule	uniform	juice	blue
cute	music		
huge	ukulele		
cube			

$\bar{u}$

©2004 by Evan-Moor Corp. • Basic Phonics Skills, Level C • EMC 3320

A cute mule
in a blue uniform
drinks juice.

A cute mule
in a blue uniform
sits on a huge cube.

4

5

Basic Phonics Skills, Level C • EMC 3320 • ©2004 by Evan-Moor Corp.

fold 2

fold 2

fold 1

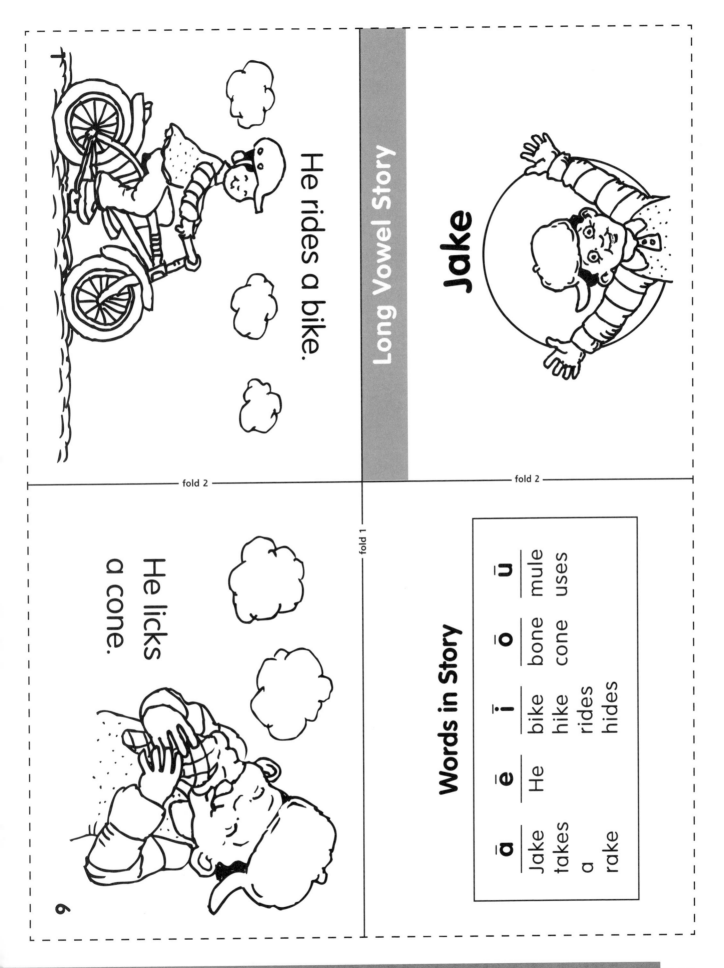

He rides a bike.

Jake

He licks
a cone.

6

Words in Story

ā	ē	ī	ō	ū
Jake	He	bike	bone	mule
takes		hike	cone	uses
a		rides		
rake		hides		

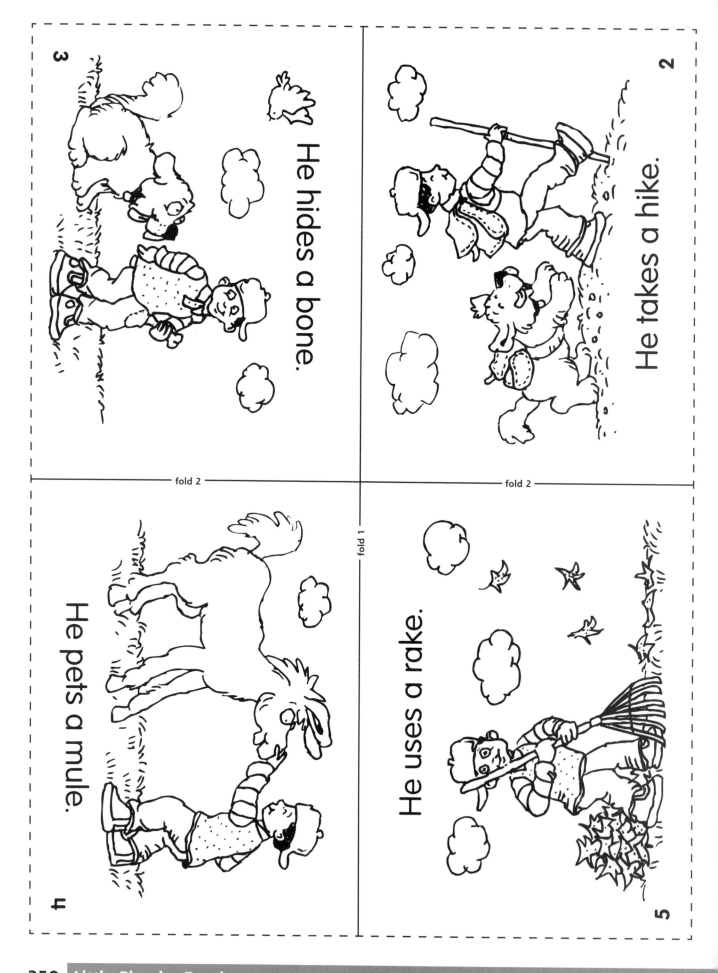

3

He hides a bone.

2

He takes a hike.

He pets a mule.

4

He uses a rake.

5

1

A Cake for Mike

Kate made a cake.

He likes the plane, too.   6

Words in Story

ā	ē	ī
Kate plane gave	He	Mike
made	She	like
a		likes
cake		

3

It is like a plane.

2

It is for Mike.

fold 2

fold 1

fold 2

She gave Mike a plane.

4

Mike likes the cake.

5

Basic Phonics Skills, Level C • EMC 3320 • ©2004 by Evan-Moor Corp.

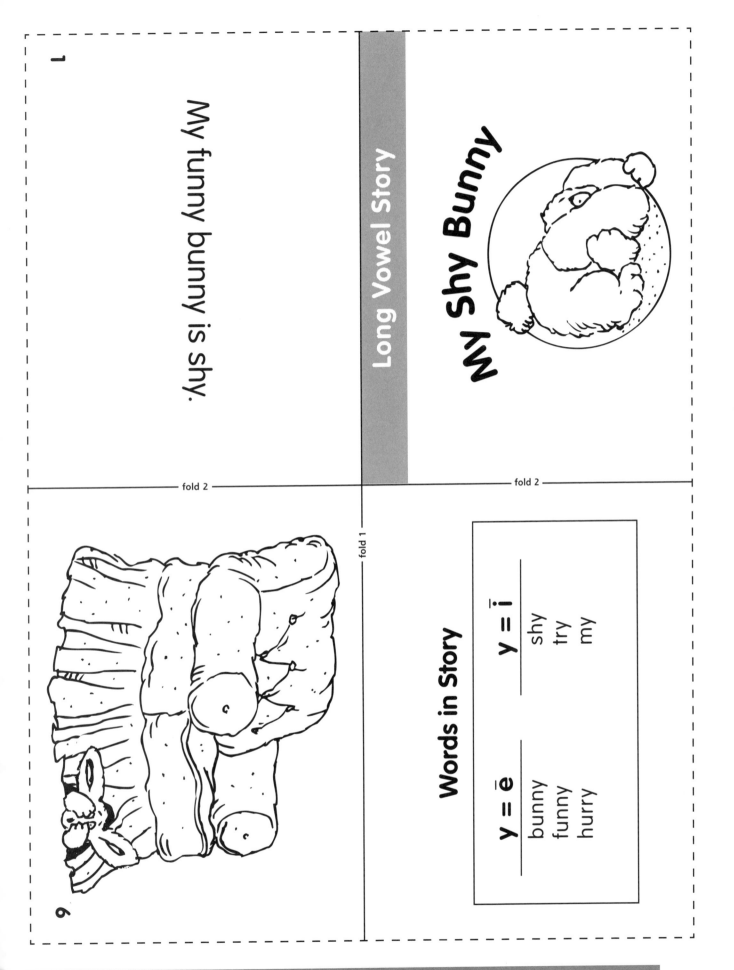

1

My funny bunny is shy.

My Shy Bunny

Words in Story

y = ē	y = ī
bunny	shy
funny	try
hurry	my

6

3

Hurry, bunny.
Try to hide.

fold 2

2

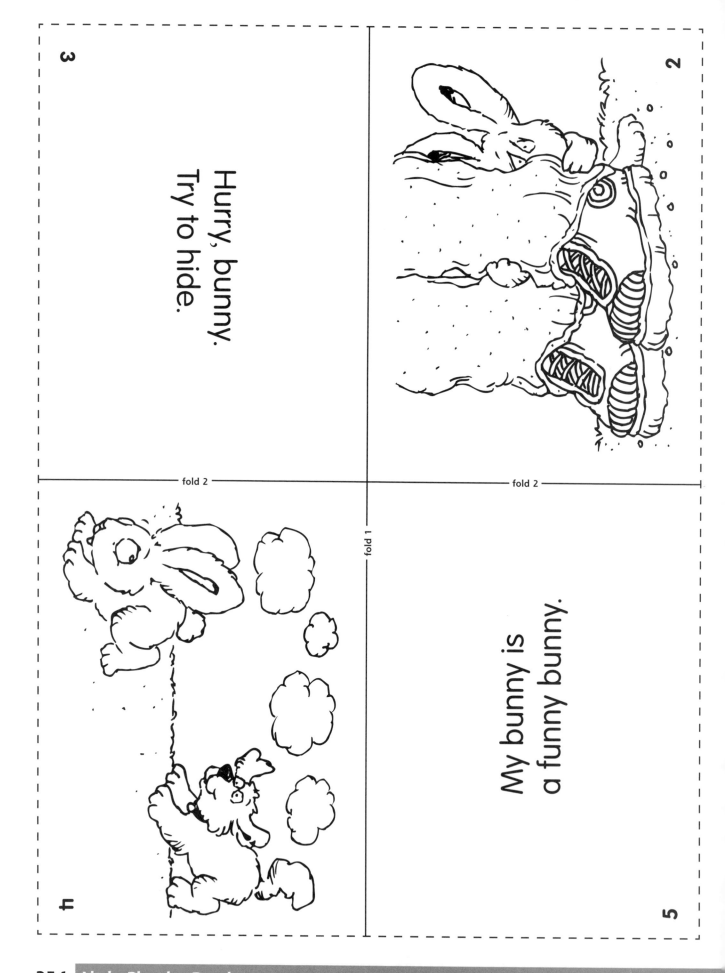

fold 1

fold 2

My bunny is
a funny bunny.

4

5

Basic Phonics Skills, Level C • EMC 3320 • ©2004 by Evan-Moor Corp.

Word Family -ame

Flame and Tame

1

Her name is Flame.

6

Tame says, "It's a shame."

Words in Story

Flame
name
lame
shame
Tame

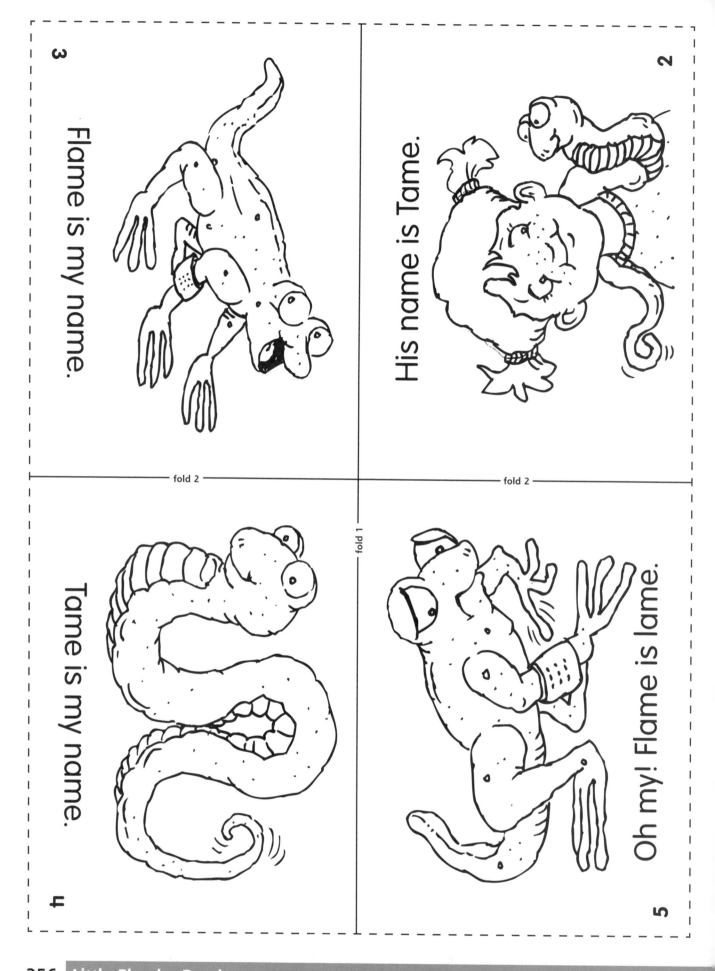

3

Flame is my name.

2

His name is Tame.

fold 2

fold 1

fold 2

4

Tame is my name.

5

Oh my! Flame is lame.

Basic Phonics Skills, Level C • EMC 3320 • ©2004 by Evan-Moor Corp.

1

Goat floats.

Word Family –oat

Goat

fold 2

fold 2

fold 1

6

Goat eats oats.

Words in Story

goat
floats
boat
coat
oats

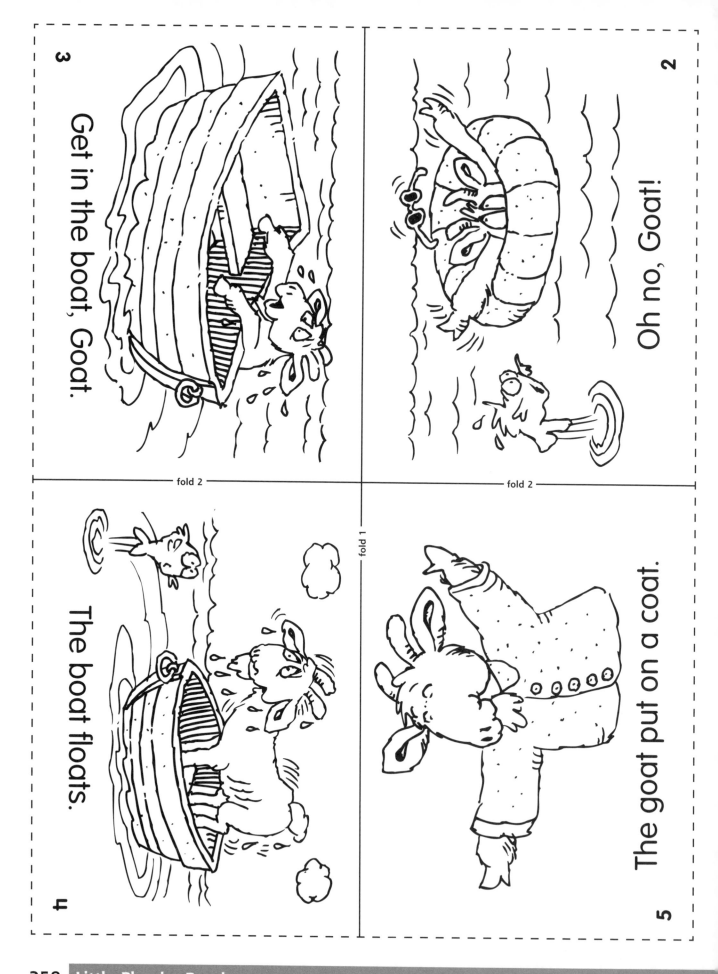

3

Get in the boat, Goat.

2

Oh no, Goat!

fold 2

fold 2

fold 1

4

The boat floats.

5

The goat put on a coat.

x

Basic Phonics Skills, Level C • EMC 3320 • ©2004 by Evan-Moor Corp.

1

seat

Word Family -eat

Repeat...

fold 2

fold 2

fold 1

Treat!
Neat!
Let's eat!

Words in Story

seat	treat
repeat	neat
meat	eat

6

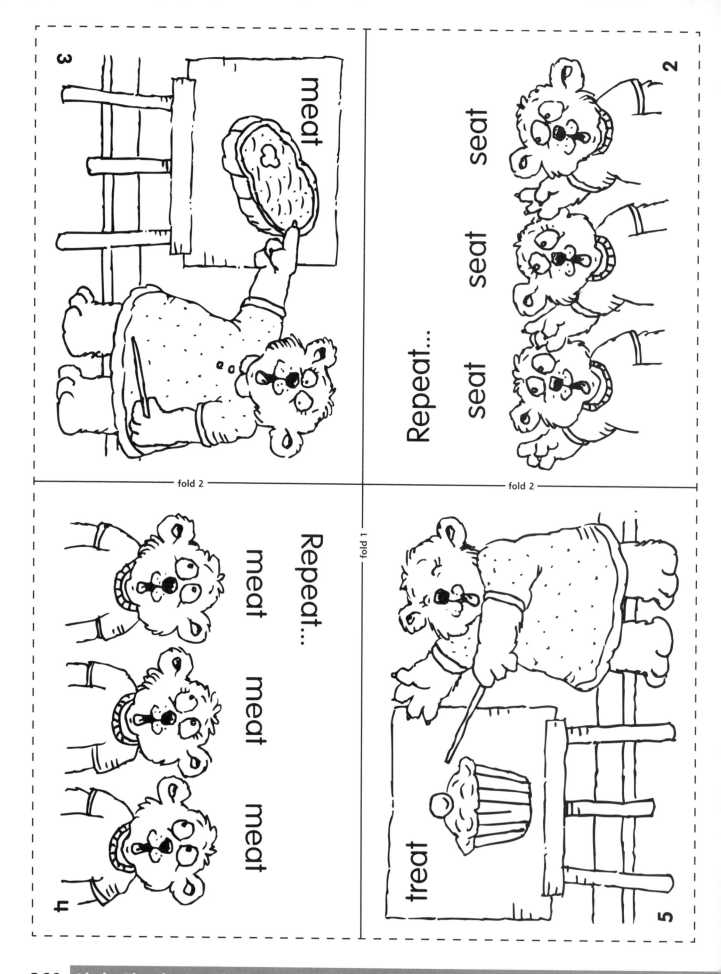

seat seat seat

Repeat...

2

meat

3

Repeat...

meat meat meat

4

treat

5

1

No Longer Alone

fold 2 —— fold 2

fold 1

I got a bone.
It was under the stone.

No longer alone!

Words in Story

alone
stone
bone
cone

6

3

I am alone.
I have a cone.

2

I am alone.
I have no bone.

4

5

Basic Phonics Skills, Level C • EMC 3320 • ©2004 by Evan-Moor Corp.

1

It is night.
The light is bright.
See the knight.

In the Night

Words in Story

night	knight
fight	right
light	sight
bright	tonight

6

fold 2

fold 1

fold 2

3

What a sight!
Will the knight fight?

2

Not tonight!
It will be all right.

5

4

Basic Phonics Skills, Level C • EMC 3320 • ©2004 by Evan-Moor Corp.

1

Nine fine swine

Fine Swine

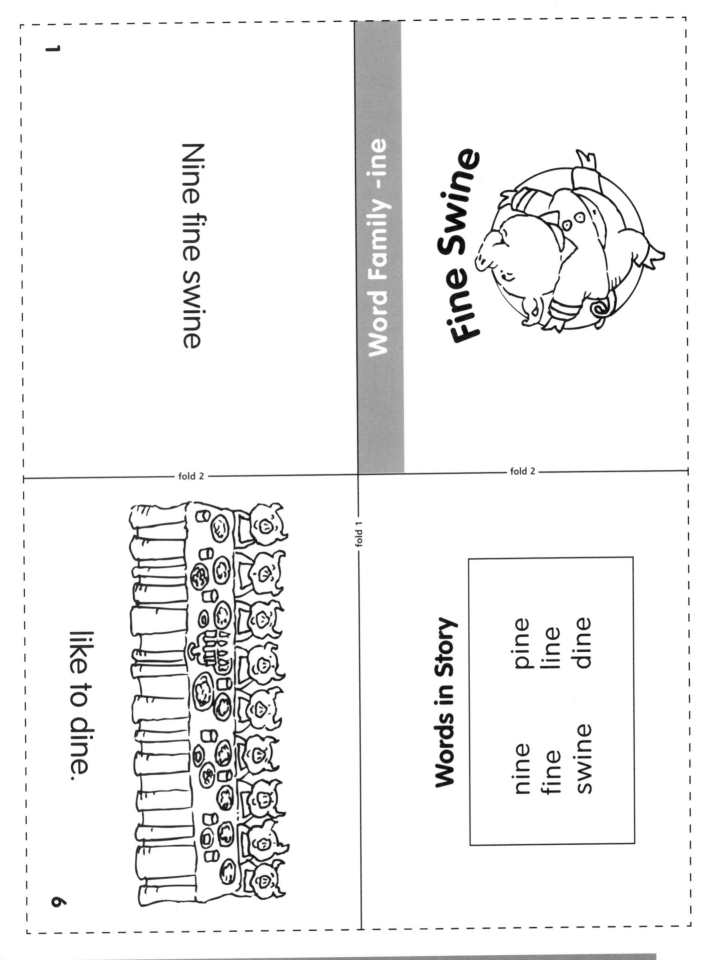

like to dine.

6

Words in Story

nine	pine
fine	line
swine	dine

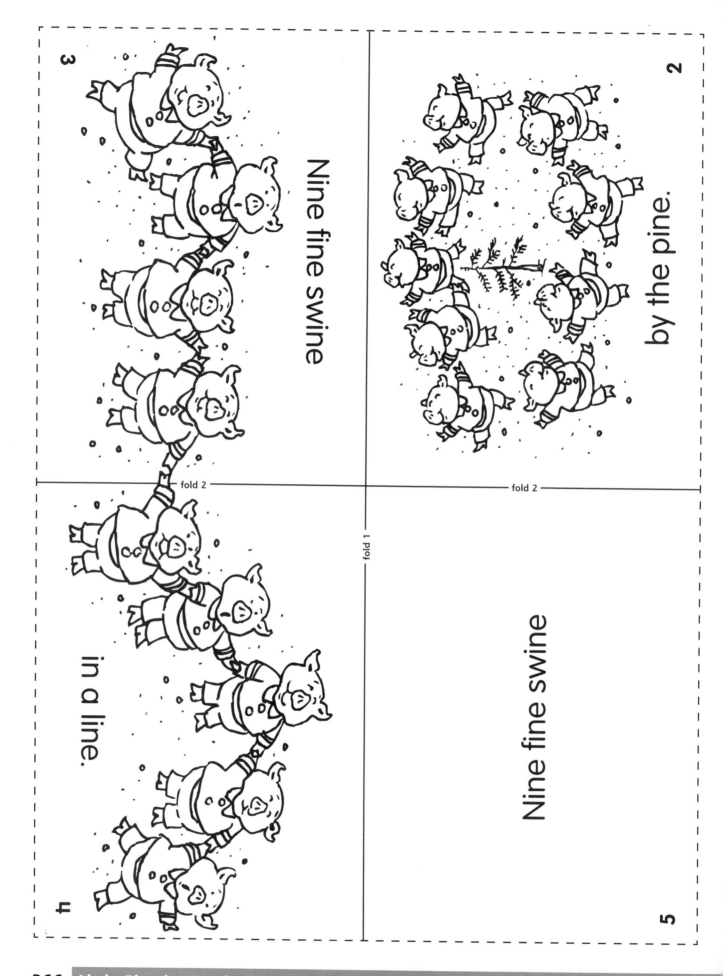

3

Nine fine swine

2

by the pine.

fold 2

fold 2

fold 1

in a line.

4

Nine fine swine

5

Basic Phonics Skills, Level C • EMC 3320 • ©2004 by Evan-Moor Corp.

side by Side

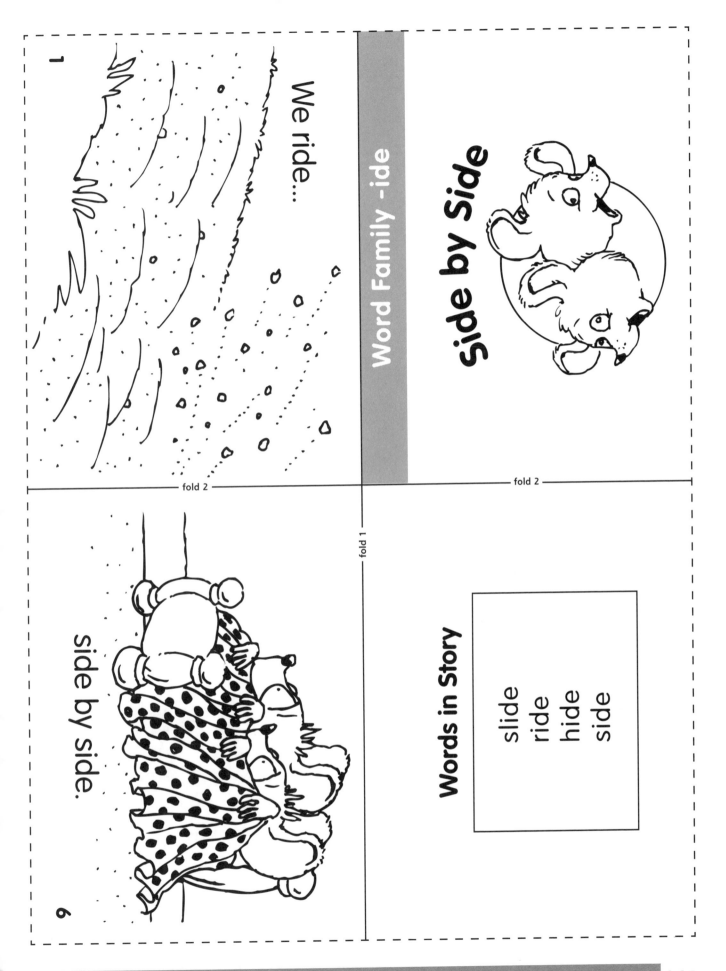

1

We ride...

side by side.

6

Words in Story

slide
ride
hide
side

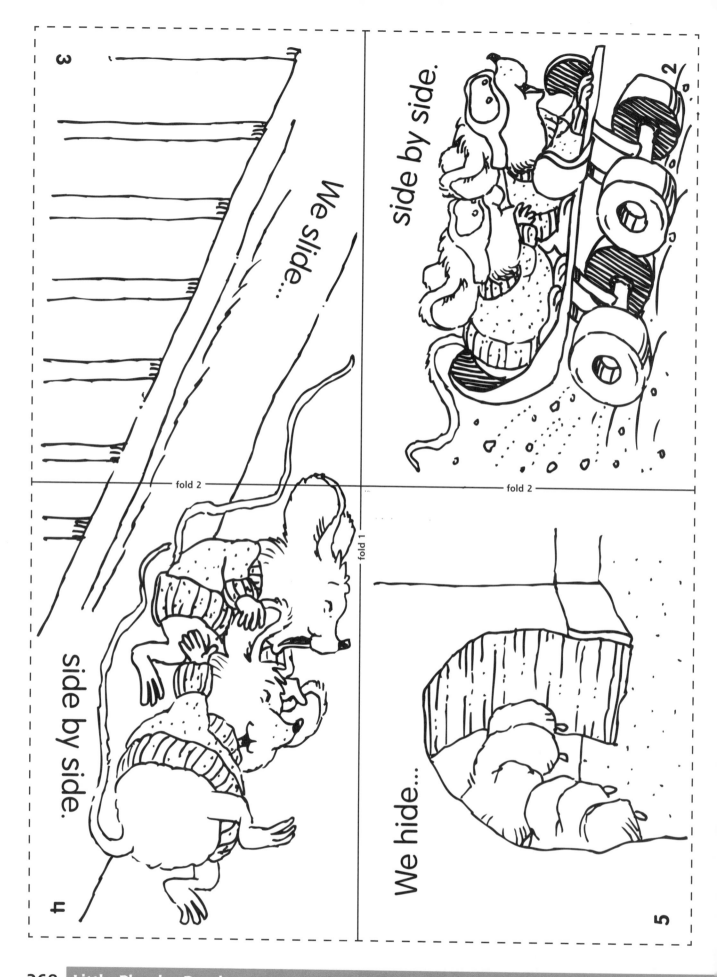

side by side.

2

side by side.

3

side by side.

4

We hide...

5

We slide...

fold 2

fold 1

fold 2

1

Will Kay lay eggs today?

Will Kay Lay?

No, Kay will stay.

Hooray!

6

Words in Story

Kay	away
lay	hooray
hay	stay
may	today

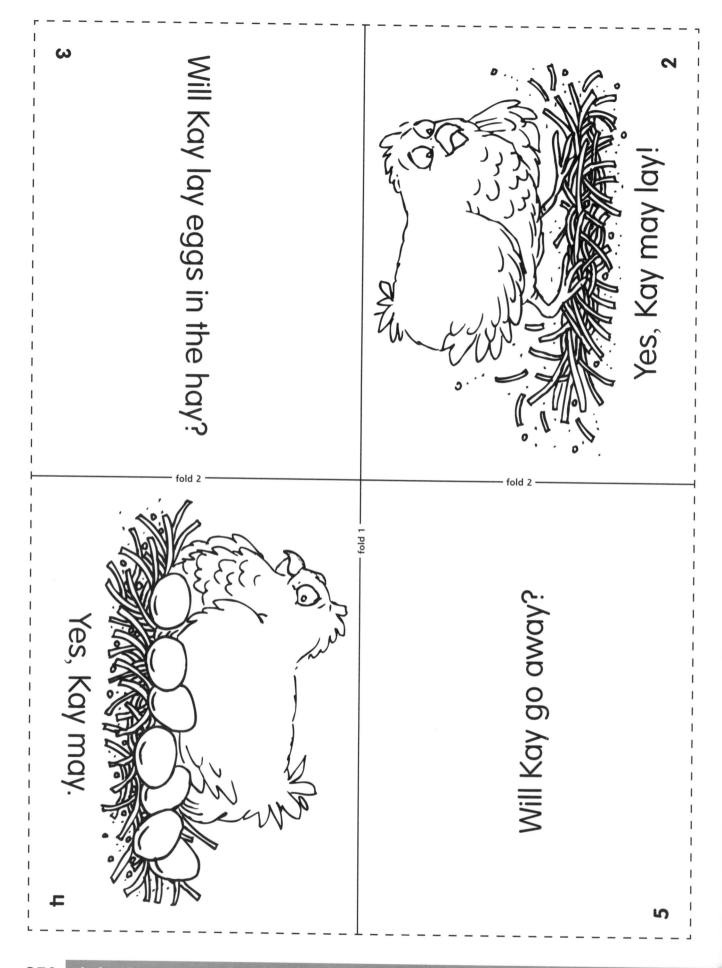

3

Will Kay lay eggs in the hay?

2

Yes, Kay may lay!

4

Yes, Kay may.

5

Will Kay go away?

Basic Phonics Skills, Level C • EMC 3320 • ©2004 by Evan-Moor Corp.

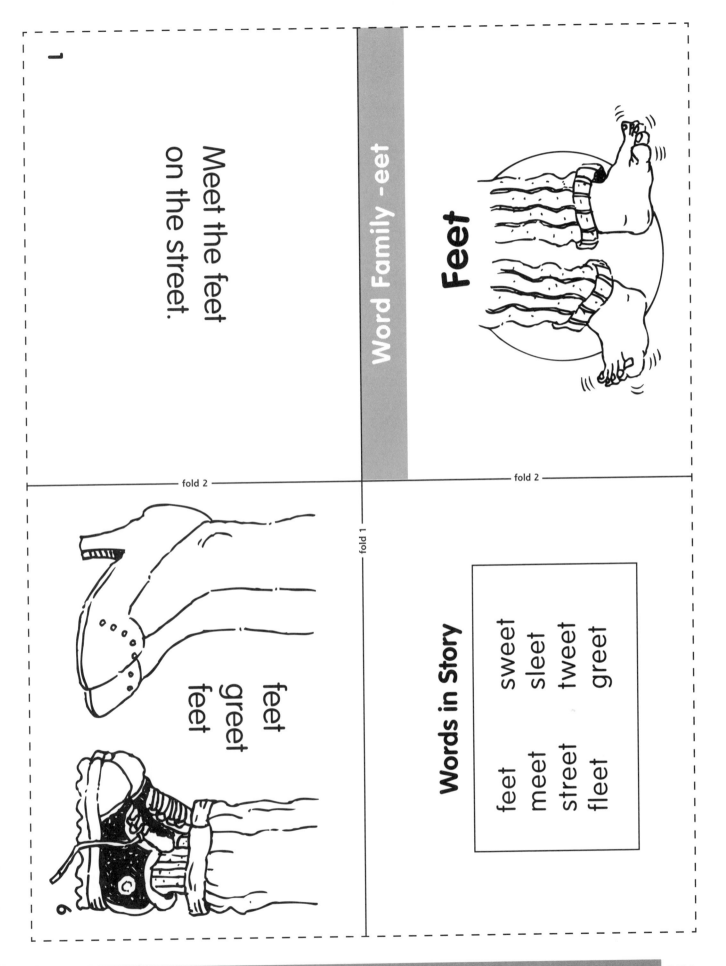

Word Family -eet

Feet

1

Meet the feet
on the street.

Words in Story

feet	sweet
meet	sleet
street	tweet
fleet	greet

feet
greet
feet

6

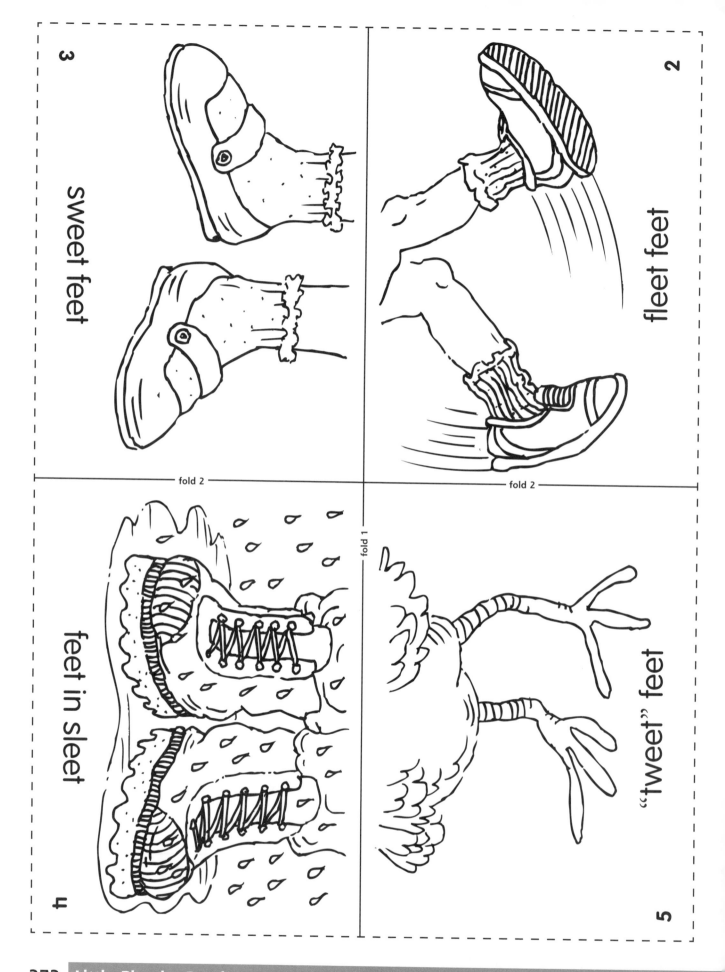

3

sweet feet

2

fleet feet

4

feet in sleet

5

"tweet" feet

fold 2

fold 2

fold 1

Basic Phonics Skills, Level C • EMC 3320 • ©2004 by Evan-Moor Corp.

1

It's
a
leak!

speak, Mouse

---

creak

6

Words in Story

leak	creak
tweak	squeak
streak	speak

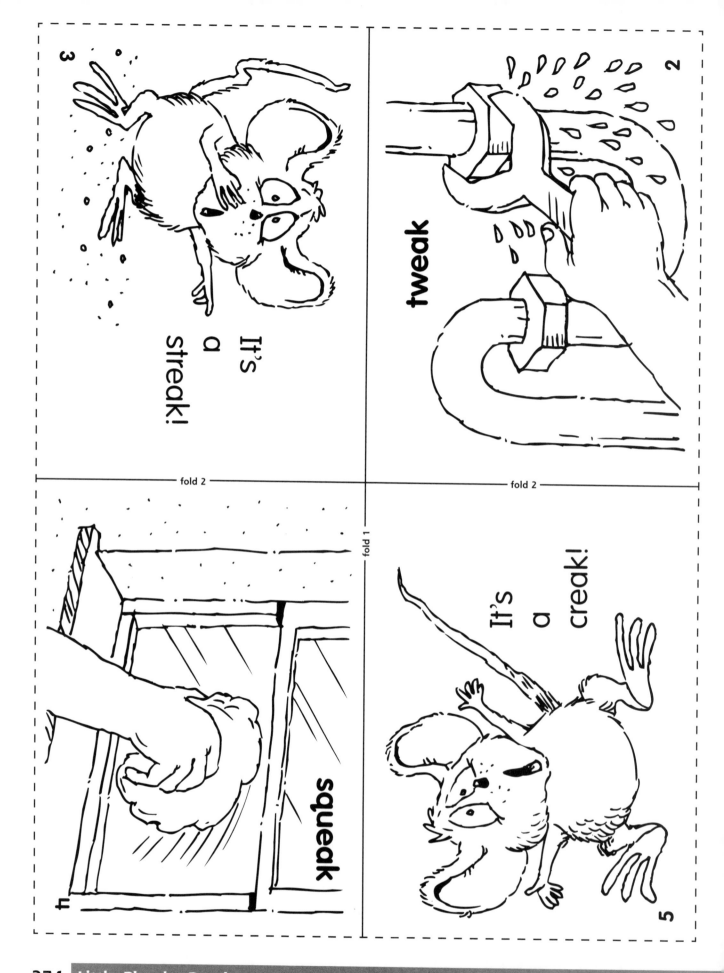

3

It's
a
streak!

tweak

2

squeak

H

It's
a
creak!

5

fold 2

fold 2

fold 1

Ruff was old,
but he was bold.

Bold Ruff

Words in Story

	gold
	hold
	told
bold	
old	
cold	

6

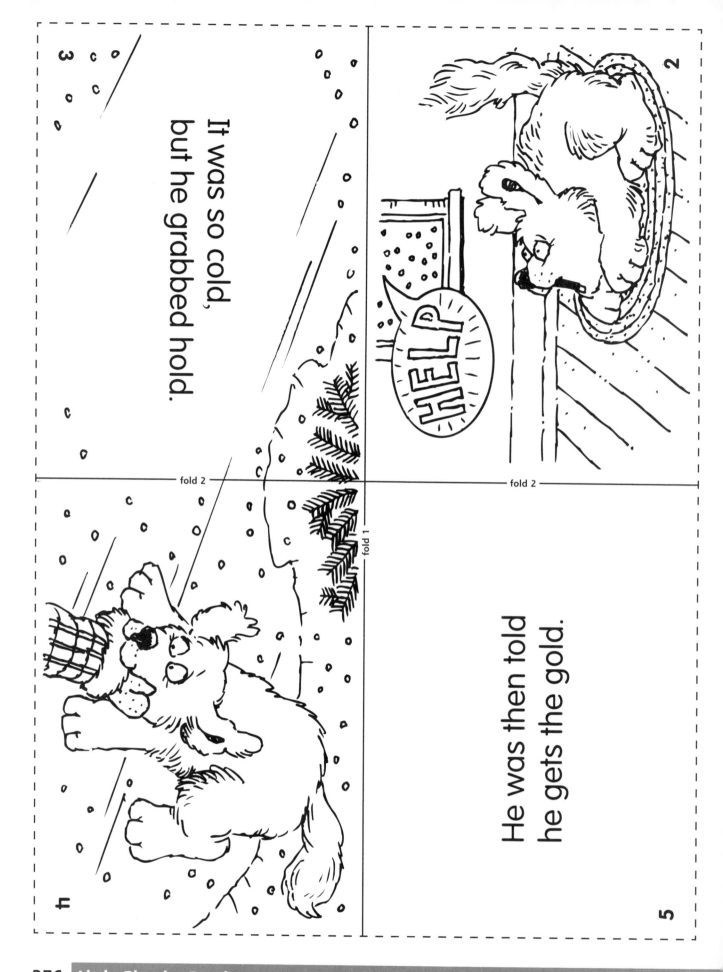

3

It was so cold,
but he grabbed hold.

2

HELP

4

He was then told
he gets the gold.

5

seed Surprise

Do you see a seed?

1

Indeed! 6

Words in Story

seed	need
indeed	feed
weed	

Will it need to feed?

3

Indeed. **2**

Indeed. **4**

Oh no! It's a weed!

5

Basic Phonics Skills, Level C • EMC 3320 • ©2004 by Evan-Moor Corp.

Answer Key

Page 9   Circled: tape, plate, cage, gate, skates, chain

Page 10   Students draw lines from the map, cat, fan, and man to the **apple**; students draw lines from the vase, cane, snake, and whale to the **ape**.

Page 11   Students match ape, snake, plate, and gate to their pictures; 1. plate; 2. snake; 3. gate; 4. ape

Page 12   1. snake; 2. plate; 3. gate; 4. cage; 5. vase; 6. Jake

Page 13   Circled: he, we, she, bee, and 3

Page 14   Students draw lines from the pen, leg, bed, and hen to the **jet**; students draw lines from the tea, tree, bean, and we to **me**.

Page 15   **e:** he, she, be; **ee:** bee, Lee, see; 1. see; 2. bee; 3. be

Page 16   1. tree; 2. Three; 3. see; 4. bees; 5. Lee; 6. flee

Page 17

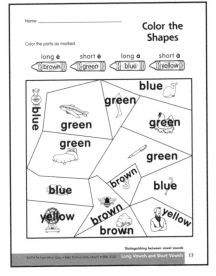

Page 18   Circled: dime, slide, 9, bike, ice, and pipe

Page 19   Students draw lines from the dice, 9, bike, pie, and pipe to the **kite**; students draw lines from the pin, wig, and fish to the **pig**.

Page 20   Students match nine, pipe, dime, and bike to their pictures; 1. dime; 2. bike; 3. nine; 4. pipe

Page 21   1. like; 2. Mike; 3. nine; 4. five; 5. ice; 6. bike

Page 22   Circled: smoke, rope, bone, soap, hoe, and toe

Page 23   Students draw lines from the hose, rose, nose, and toe to the **bone**; students draw lines from the clock, fox, sock, and stop sign to the **top**.

Page 24 Students match rose, bone, nose, and hole to their pictures; 1. rose; 2. nose; 3. bone; 4. hole

Page 25 1. rode; 2. rope; 3. hose; 4. nose; 5. hole; 6. bone

Page 26 Circled: mule, tube, uniform, and unicorn

Page 27 Students draw lines from the tube, mule, flute, and unicorn to the **cube**; students draw lines from the sub, tub, up arrow, and bug to the **cup**.

Page 28 Students match flute, tube, cube, and mule to their pictures; 1. cube; 2. tube; 3. flute; 4. mule

Page 29 1. uniforms; 2. June; 3. flute; 4. tuba; 5. tune; 6. music

Page 30 1. ā; 2. ē; 3. ī; 4. ī; 5. ā; 6. ē; 7. ī; 8. ī

Page 31 1. ō; 2. ī; 3. ū; 4. ī; 5. ō; 6. ō; 7. ū; 8. ī

Page 32 1. ē; 2. ā; 3. ī; 4. ū; 5. ō; 6. ā; 7. ē; 8. ō

Page 33 1. r**o**se; 2. bike; 3. d**i**ce; 4. t**a**pe; 5. w**e**; 6. pl**a**te; 7. nine; 8. h**o**se; 9. fl**u**te

Page 34 1. kite; 2. nine; 3. m**u**le; 4. h**e**; 5. line; 6. v**a**se; 7. sn**a**ke; 8. h**o**se; 9. b**o**ne

Page 35 1. snake; 2. slide; 3. pine; 4. smoke; 5. cube; 6. nine; 7. whale; 8. pipe; 9. tape

Page 36

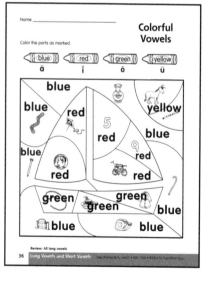

Page 37 1. code; 2. snake; 3. cube; 4. pine; 5. tape; 6. rock

Page 38 Students add e and match objects to words.

Page 39 Students add e and match objects to words.

Page 40 Students add e and match objects to words.

Page 41 Students add e and match objects to words.

Page 42 1. robe; 2. ride; 3. cute; 4. kite; 5. Tim; 6. plane

Page 43 1. dime; 2. cone; 3. ate; 4. Kit; 5. plane; 6. huge

Basic Phonics Skills, Level C • EMC 3320 • ©2004 by Evan-Moor Corp.

Page 44 1. mane; 2. cute; 3. huge; 4. bite; 5. ride; 6. hide

Page 45 1. cub; 2. cute; 3. hug; 4. us; 5. us; 6. tub

Page 47 Circled: car, cup, cage, can; cake, cup, can

Page 48 Circled: celery, circle, circus, city; circle, circus

Page 49 Students draw lines from cent, city, and circle to **cereal**; students draw lines from car, cape, candle, corn, and cup to **cake**.

Page 50 1. /k/; 2. /k/; 3. /s/; 4. /k/; 5. /s/; 6. /k/

Page 51 1. come; 2. call; 3. cents; 4. car; 5. cat; 6. cage

Page 52 Circled: giraffe, general, gingerbread; giant, gingerbread

Page 53 Circled: gum, girl, gift, gas; gate, goose

Page 54 Students draw lines from gate, girl, gum, gift, and gas to **goat**; students draw lines from gem, general, and giant to **giraffe**.

Page 55 1. /j/; 2. /g/; 3. /j/; 4. /g/; 5. /g/; 6. /j/

Page 56 1. gate; 2. giraffe; 3. goat; 4. gas; 5. game; 6. gem

Page 57 1. garden; 2. cave; 3. circle; 4. cab; 5. come; 6. gem

Page 59 Students draw lines from thumb, 30, and thimble to **thread**; students draw lines from shirt, shapes, shell, ship, and sheep to **shoe**.

Page 60 Students draw lines from whiskers, wheel, and whistle to **whale**; students draw lines from chick, cheese, chain, chimney, and cherry to **chair**.

Page 61 1. th; 2. ch; 3. wh; 4. sh; 5. wh; 6. sh; 7. th; 8. ch

Page 62 Students draw lines from thread, 30, and thimble to **th**; students draw lines from shoe and shell to **sh**; students draw lines from whale and whistle to **wh**; students draw lines from chair, cherry, and cheese to **ch**.

Page 63 1. wh; 2. th; 3. wh; 4. sh; 5. ch; 6. ch

Page 64 tooth/bath; branch/watch; brush/fish; leash/fish; bench/watch; wreath/bath

Page 65 1. sh; 2. ch; 3. ch; 4. th; 5. ch; 6. sh; 7. th; 8. sh

Page 66 1. sh; 2. th; 3. sh; 4. th; 5. ch; 6. ch

Page 68 Students match words to their pictures.

Page 69 **er:** finger, water, ladder, over; **ur:** curl, purse, nurse, burn; **ir:** girl, first, dirt, shirt

Page 70 1. bird; 2. fir; 3. purple; 4. river; 5. water; 6. turtle; 7. over; 8. turn

Page 71 Students draw lines from star, jar, and arm to **car**; students draw lines from horn, horse, and north to **fork**.

Page 72 1. ar; 2. ar; 3. or; 4. ar; 5. or; 6. ar; 7. or; 8. or

Page 73 1. c**ar**; 2. st**ar**; 3. h**or**se; 4. **jar**; 5. c**or**n; 6. y**ar**n; 7. **ar**m; 8. f**or**k

Page 74 1. ar; 2. ur; 3. ir; 4. or; 5. er; 6. ar; 7. ir; 8. ur; 9. ar

Page 75 1. girl; 2. barn; 3. horse; 4. arm; 5. north; 6. river

Page 76 1. winter; 2. girl; 3. letter; 4. arms; 5. sweater; 6. warm; 7. park; 8. dark

Page 78 1. tr**ai**n; 2. ch**ai**n; 3. sn**ai**l; 4. h**ay**; 5. p**ai**l; 6. j**ay**

Page 79 1. tail; 2. snail; 3. tray; 4. hay; 5. nail; 6. pail; r**ai**l, l**ay**, tr**ay**, s**ai**l, s**ay**, h**ai**l

Page 80 pain, main, brain, gain; hay, may, say, day; 1. brain; 2. hay; 3. say; 4. pain

Page 81 1. jay; 2. train; 3. play; 4. chain; 5. sail; 6. clay

Page 82 1. Jay, paint; 2. pay; 3. gray; 4. pail; 5. play

Page 83 1. l**ea**f; 2. j**ee**p; 3. s**ea**l; 4. r**ea**d; 5. f**ee**t; 6. b**ea**n

Page 84 1. beet; 2. sea; 3. pea; 4. cheek; 5. peek; 6. feet; m**ee**t, t**ea**m, t**ea**, fl**ea**, w**ee**k, m**ea**n

Page 85 1. sea; 2. we; 3. pea; 4. beet; 5. bean; 6. feet

Page 86 beep, peep, keep, deep; deal, heal, meal, real; 1. jeep; 2. seal

Page 87 1. jeep; 2. beans; 3. feet; 4. seed; 5. bee; 6. seal

Page 88 1. beat; 2. neat; 3. Please, sleep; 4. jeep; 5. street; 6. dream

Page 89 1. l**igh**t; 2. t**ie**; 3. r**igh**t; 4. fr**igh**t; 5. l**ie**; 6. n**igh**t

Page 90 1. tie; 2. light; 3. night; 4. pie; 5. right; 6. knight; l**ie**, br**igh**t, s**igh**t, f**igh**t, m**igh**t, d**ie**

Page 91 1. l**ie**; 2. p**ie**; 3. l**igh**t; 4. n**igh**t; 5. th**igh**; 6. t**ie**

Page 92 die, tie, lie; sight, light, tight, right; 1. right; 2. pie; 3. tight

Page 93 1. night; 2. time; 3. pine; 4. light; 5. pie; 6. tie

Page 94 1. night; 2. high; 3. light; 4. sight

Page 95 1. b**ow**; 2. c**oa**t; 3. h**oe**; 4. cr**ow**; 5. t**oa**d; 6. g**oa**t

Page 96 1. toe; 2. goat; 3. boat; 4. snow; 5. mow; 6. hoe; d**oe**, fl**oa**t, J**oe**, kn**ow**, m**oa**t, l**ow**

Page 97 1. b**oa**t; 2. t**oa**d; 3. g**oa**t; 4. sn**ow**; 5. cr**ow**; 6. J**oe**

Page 98 doe, foe, hoe; goat, moat, coat; mow, tow, row; 1. hoe; 2. boat; 3. bow

Page 99 1. goat; 2. toad; 3. snow; 4. toe; 5. coach; 6. bow

Page 100 1. Joe, coat; 2. load; 3. road; 4. snow; 5. tow

Page 101 fruit, suit; blue, glue, Sue; pool, cool, tool; S**ue**, sch**oo**l, gl**ue**, bl**ue**, s**ui**t, t**oo**l

Page 102 Students match words to pictures; 1. glue; 2. suit; 3. stool; 4. pool

Page 103   1. glue; 2. school; 3. fruit; 4. pool; **Sue, roo**m, sch**ool**, p**ool**

Page 104   1. g**oo**se; 2. j**ui**ce; 3. gl**ue**; bl**ue**, st**ool**, c**ool**, j**ui**ce

Page 105   1. suit; 2. blue; 3. juice; 4. zoom; 5. boots; 6. due

Page 106   1. moose, loose, zoo; 2. scoop, food, Sue; 3. soon; 4. loop

Page 107   Students draw lines from cry, fry, and why to **fly**; students draw lines from happy, lady, and bunny to **sunny**.

Page 108   1. ī; 2. ē; 3. ē; 4. ī; 5. ē; 6. ē; 7. ī; 8. ē

Page 109   1. ī, 1; 2. ī, 1; 3. ē, 2; 4. ī, 1; 5. ē, 2; 6. ē, 2; 7. ī, 1; 8. ē, 2; ī, ē

Page 110   1. baby; 2. cry; 3. sky; 4. Why; 5. bunny; 6. happy

Page 111   1. Sunny; 2. funny; 3. pony; 4. penny; 5. why; 6. sky

Page 112   1. l**igh**t; 2. p**ea**; 3. s**ea**t; 4. bab**y**; 5. p**ie**; 6. f**ee**t; 7. b**ee**t; 8. fl**y**; 9. t**ie**

Page 113   **Under ē**: team, sunny, bee, meal, greet, tree; **under ī**: by, light, sight, pie, sky, high

Page 114   1. meal, free, deal; 2. tight, fright; 3. lean, clean; 4. cry, good-bye; 5. funny, puppy, fly

Page 115   **Long e (ea, ee, y) words circled:** Bunny, needed, greens, eat, Baby, leave, meet, see, neat, and funny; **Long i (ie, igh, y) words underlined:** Fright, Sky, Lie, might, fright, sights, My, tried, right, sight, and night

Page 116   1. b**oa**t; 2. t**ai**l; 3. gl**ue**; 4. s**ui**t; 5. b**ow**l; 6. h**ay**; 7. b**oo**t; 8. g**oa**l; 9. h**oe**

Page 117   **Under ā**: grain, afraid, pray, wait, trail, clay; **under ō**: toes, woe, float, moan, flow, blow; **under ōō**: spoon, suit, hoot, clue, fruit, loon

Page 118   1. stay, train; 2. blow, rain; 3. hoe, fruit; 4. boat, toots, soon; 5. blue, suit

Page 119   **Long a (ai, ay) words circled:** bay, stay, sailing, away; **Long o (oa, ow) words underlined:** snow, roam, boat, stow, floating; **oo (ue, ui, oo) words X'd:** Blue, Goose, suit, soon

Page 120   1. tie; 2. pie; 3. pea; 4. bow; 5. fruit; 6. boat; 7. tail; 8. bee; 9. hay

Page 121   1. root, toe; 2. daylight, fleet; 3. tray, soap; 4. might, tie; 5. bait, treat

Page 122   **Under ā**: A, ate, may; **under ē**: meet, we, each, leave, he; **under ī**: Night, I, my, find; **under ō**: show, both, so, coat, go, low; **under ōō**: Sue, blue, fruit, loops, to, suit

Page 124   **sl**ed, **st**ar, **sw**ing, **sk**ull

Page 125   1. sl; 2. st; 3. sk; 4. sw; 5. sl; 6. st; 7. st; 8. sk

Page 126   1. **st**ove; 2. **sw**im; 3. **sk**unk; 4. **sl**ide; 5. **sk**ates; 6. **st**op; 7. **sl**ed; 8. **sw**an; 9. **st**ick

Page 127   1. sweep; 2. sled; 3. swim; 4. stop; 5. stick; 6. skull

Page 128 1. stamp; 2. stove; 3. swan; 4. star; 5. sky; 6. store; 7. sweep; 8. steps

Page 129 **sn**ail; **sp**oon, **sm**oke, **sc**are

Page 130 1. sn; 2. sp; 3. sc; 4. sn; 5. sm; 6. sp; 7. sc; 8. sm (smell) or sn (sniff)

Page 131 1. **sp**ace; 2. **sp**ool; 3. **sn**ap; 4. **sm**ile; 5. **sn**ail; 6. **sc**ale; 7. **sp**ill; 8. **sn**ake; 9. **sc**oop

Page 132 1. snail; 2. smoke; 3. spoon; 4. spill; 5. spider; 6. scare; 7. scoop; 8. spot; 9. snake

Page 133 1. spoon; 2. score; 3. spider; 4. snow; 5. space; 6. smells; 7. snail; 8. smile

Page 134 1. She can smell; 2. She can swim; 3. Here is a sled; 4. It is a slide.

Page 135 1. steps; 2. smoke; 3. snow; 4. scare; 5. skunk; 6. spill; 7. slip; 8. swan

Page 136 **cl**own, **gl**obe, **fl**y, **gl**ue

Page 137 1. cl; 2. fl; 3. fl; 4. gl; 5. gl; 6. cl; 7. cl; 8. fl

Page 138 1. **cl**own; 2. **gl**ue; 3. **fl**ute; 4. **cl**ap; 5. **cl**ock; 6. **gl**ass; 7. **fl**ag; 8. **cl**oud; 9. **gl**ove

Page 139 1. flag; 2. glad; 3. clap; 4. globe; 5. flame; 6. flute; 7. clown; 8. clock; 9. glue

Page 140 1. clown; 2. flute; 3. gloves; 4. class; 5. flag; 6. cloudy; 7. floor; 8. glad

Page 141 **pl**ant, **bl**oom, **pl**ug, **bl**anket

Page 142 1. **pl**um; 2. **bl**ack; 3. **pl**ant; 4. **bl**ock; 5. **gl**ue; 6. **pl**ane; 7. **pl**ate; 8. **gl**ove; 9. **bl**ink

Page 143 Answers will vary.

Page 144 1. play; 2. blade; 3. plug; 4. block; 5. plant; 6. blow

Page 145 1. plant; 2. block; 3. plane; 4. planet; 5. plum; 6. blue; 7. blow; 8. black

Page 146 1. I love red plums; 2. The clock is here; 3. The snail is on the plant; 4. The bloom is big.

Page 147 1. clown; 2. play; 3. blue; 4. flag; 5. plant; 6. clear; 7. glass; 8. clock

Page 148 **gr**apes, **cr**ow, **fr**ame, **cr**ab

Page 149 1. fr; 2. fr; 3. gr; 4. cr; 5. cr; 6. cr; 7. fr; 8. gr

Page 150 1. **cr**ow; 2. **fr**og; 3. **fr**ame; 4. **gr**apes; 5. **fr**uit; 6. **gr**ay; 7. **gr**ill; 8. **cr**ab; 9. **cr**oss

Page 151 1. grin; 2. crown; 3. fruit; 4. frame; 5. grass; 6. crawl; 7. frown; 8. crow; 9. cross

Page 152 1. crow; 2. grow; 3. cross; 4. cry; 5. crown; 6. frame; 7. creek; 8. from

Page 153 **dr**ip, **pr**ice, **br**ush, **tr**ee

Page 154 1. br; 2. tr; 3. dr; 4. pr; 5. br; 6. dr; 7. pr; 8. tr

Page 155 1. **tr**uck; 2. **dr**ink; 3. **tr**ee; 4. **dr**um; 5. **br**aid; 6. **pr**ize; 7. **br**ick; 8. **pr**esent; 9. **tr**ay

Page 156 1. prize; 2. drum; 3. truck; 4. dress; 5. bridge; 6. bread

Page 157 1. train; 2. prune; 3. drum; 4. press; 5. prize; 6. tree; 7. drew; 8. dress

Page 158 1. The truck stopped; 2. The dress is pretty; 3. The queen has a crown;
4. She has one braid.

Page 159 1. brick; 2. grass; 3. trip; 4. dress; 5. grapes; 6. frog; 7. cry; 8. dry

Page 160 **tw**ins, **qu**arter, **qu**ail, **tw**elve, **qu**ack

Page 161 1. tw; 2. qu; 3. qu; 4. qu; 5. tw; 6. tw; 7. qu; 8. tw

Page 162 1. twins; 2. quilt; 3. quack; 4. twig; 5. quail; 6. twelve; 7. queen; 8. twenty;
9. quarter

Page 163 1. star; 2. snail; 3. sled; 4. flag; 5. glass; 6. plant; 7. crow; 8. spoon

Page 164 1. skunk; 2. spider; 3. click; 4. blocks; 5. crown; 6. train

Page 165 cla**sp**, de**sk**, fi**st**, cru**st**

Page 166 1. st; 2. st; 3. st; 4. sk; 5. st; 6. sk; 7. sp; 8. st

Page 167 1. ve**st**; 2. wri**st**; 3. de**sk**; 4. ne**st**; 5. li**st**; 6. ma**sk**; 7. toa**st**; 8. wa**sp**; 9. fi**st**

Page 168 1. desk; 2. clasp; 3. mask; 4. vest; 5. wrist; 6. blast; 7. toast; 8. wasp; 9. nest

Page 169 1. nest; 2. roast; 3. wasp; 4. fist; 5. mask; 6. crust; 7. wrist

Page 170 Students should mark beginning circles for star, skunk, skirt, spider, and
spoon; students should mark ending circles for nest, vest, mask, and wasp.

Page 171 **Beginning:** star, skunk, spider; **Ending:** nest, desk, clasp

Page 172 g**old**, qui**lt**, she**lf**, sa**lt**

Page 173 1. ld; 2. lt; 3. lt; 4. lf; 5. ld; 6. lt; 7. lf; 8. lt

Page 174 1. co**lt**; 2. fo**ld**; 3. wo**lf**; 4. co**ld**; 5. qui**lt**; 6. be**lt**; 7. sa**lt**; 8. go**lf**; 9. ho**ld**

Page 175 1. shelf; 2. golf; 3. belt; 4. gold; 5. elf; 6. melt

Page 176 1. cold; 2. quilt; 3. told; 4. gold; 5. felt; 6. held

Page 177 1. The bird is in its nest; 2. My belt is big; 3. My desk is clean;
4. The books are on the shelf.

Page 178 1. elf, quilt; 2. wasp, wrist; 3. golf, vest; 4. salt, roast; 5. colt; 6. desk, fist;
7. shelf

Page 179 dri**nk**, pla**nt**, sa**nd**, pai**nt**

Page 180 1. nk; 2. nt; 3. nt; 4. nk; 5. nt; 6. nd; 7. nd; 8. nk

Page 181 1. sa**nd**; 2. te**nt**; 3. ce**nt**; 4. ha**nd**; 5. tru**nk**; 6. ba**nk**; 7. pai**nt**; 8. ba**nd**; 9. wi**nk**

Page 182 1. hand; 2. drink; 3. plant; 4. cent; 5. sink; 6. paint; 7. bank; 8. trunk; 9. sand

Page 183 1. went; 2. tent; 3. spent; 4. wind; 5. bank; 6. sand; 7. think; 8. mind

Page 184 ju**mp**, so**ft**, gi**ft**, hu**mp**

Page 185 1. mp; 2. ft; 3. mp; 4. mp; 5. ft; 6. ft; 7. mp; 8. mp

Page 186 1. hu**mp**; 2. stu**mp**; 3. ju**mp**; 4. gi**ft**; 5. ra**ft**; 6. le**ft**; 7. bli**mp**; 8. li**ft**; 9. cha**mp**

Page 187 1. gift; 2. raft; 3. camp; 4. stump; 5. ramp; 6. lamp; 7. gift; 8. left

Page 188 1. lamp, jumped; 2. camp; 3. left; 4. raft, ramp; 5. swamp; 6. swift; 7. drift

Page 189 1. stamp; 2. raft; 3. lamp; 4. trunk; 5. tent; 6. hand; 7. paint; 8. gift

Page 190 1. spent; 2. grind; 3. grant; 4. thump; 5. swift; 6. skunk; 7. stomp; 8. dunk

Page 191 1. I like your mask; 2. Turn off the lamp; 3. The bird is in the nest. Circle: wasp, mask, lamp, Don't, raft, nest, and shelf. Cross out: -ld, -lt, -nd, -nk, and -ng.

Page 192 1. wind; 2. cent; 3. colt; 4. sink; 5. crisp; 6. shelf; 7. hold, hand; 8. last, mask, left

Page 194 1. cup; 2. cups, 3. pan; 4. pans; 5. can; 6. cans; 7. top; 8. tops

Page 195 1. glasses; 2. foxes; 3. inches; 4. buses; Sentences will vary.

Page 196 **Under hats:** beds, plates, cars, pigs; **under dress<u>es</u>:** dishes, inches, wishes, boxes; 1. inches; 2. dishes <u>or</u> plates

Page 197 1. bunnies; 2. cherries; 3. fairies; 1. cherries; 2. bunnies; 3. fairies

Page 198 **Under hat<u>s</u>:** cups, eggs, hens; **under dish<u>es</u>:** inches, wishes, boxes; **under poni<u>es</u>:** ladies, babies, bunnies; 1. eggs; 2. boxes <u>or</u> cups; 3. bunnies

Page 199 1. chairs; 2. pans; 3. dishes; 4. ladies; 5. dresses; 6. inches; 7. foxes; 8. clocks

Page 200 1. jumping; 2. played; 3. jumps; 4. waiting; 5. wanted; 6. looks; 7. licking; 8. called

Page 201 1. walked; 2. wants; 3. working; 4. picking; 5. turned; 6. pulling; 7. jumped; 8. played

Page 202 sliced, slicing; poked, poking; liked, liking; taped, taping; hiked, hiking; 1. hiked; 2. taped; 3. slicing

Page 204 1. 2; 2. 3; 3. 1; 4. 3; 5. 1; 6. 2; 7. 2; 8. 1; 9. 3

Page 205

Basic Phonics Skills, Level C • EMC 3320 • ©2004 by Evan-Moor Corp.

Page 206 **1 syllable:** hand, truck, block, box; **2 syllables:** baby, away, sister, funny; **3 syllables:** butterfly, telephone, family, Saturday

Page 207

bunny	nibble	red	hill
goat	cupcake	puppy	ball
fast	seed	yellow	happy
ten	sun	snake	sunny

1. yellow; 2. happy; 3. nibble

Page 208

dinosaur	butterfly	pancake	five
after	grandmother	swing	silly
family	pajamas	better	bubble
Saturday	hill	orange	pink
wonderful	telephone	everything	octopus

1. dinosaur; 2. grandmother; 3. Saturday

Page 211 1. name; 2. goat; 3. seat; 4. flame; 5. float; 6. meat; 7. frame; 8. boat

Page 212 **Flame:** game, name, fame, came; **Goat:** boat, coat, moat, float; **Wheat:** beat, heat, meat, cheat; 1. flame; 2. goat; 3. wheat

Page 213

robot

Under -ame: came, fame, name, lame; **under -oat:** coat, goat, moat, throat, float, boat; **under -eat:** feat, heat, seat, beat, meat

Page 214 1. came; 2. seat; 3. goat; 4. game; 5. coat; 6. beat

Page 215 1. came, game; 2. boat, float; 3. treat, meat; Answers will vary.

Page 216 1. goat, tame; 2. games; 3. eat, bleat; 4. oats; 5. neat

Page 218 1. cone; 2. light; 3. line; 4. bone; 5. night; 6. nine; 7. stone; 8. right

Page 219 **Bone:** cone, tone, zone, lone; **Light:** fight, right, sight, night; **Nine:** dine, fine, line, mine; 1. bone; 2. light; 3. nine

Page 220

dog

Under -ine: nine, line, fine, mine, pine, vine; **under -ight:** right, tight, might, light, sight, bright, night, fight, flight, slight; **under -one:** cone, bone

Page 221 1. zone; 2. light; 3. fine; 4. tone; 5. might; 6. nine

Page 222 1. alone; 2. fight; 3. knight; 4. dine; 5. bone; 6. sight

Page 223 1. bone; 2. night; 3. dine; Answers will vary.

Page 225 1. hay; 2. bride; 3. feet; 4. slide; 5. gray; 6. beet; 7. tray; 8. sheet

Page 226 **Slide:** ride, side, tide, wide; **Hay:** bay, day, ray, may; **Beet:** feet, meet, fleet, greet; 1. hay; 2. beet; 3. slide

Page 227 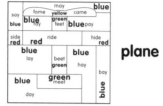 plane

Under -ay: may, pay, ray, say, hay, bay, lay; **under -ame:** fame, came; **under -eet:** feet, beet, meet; **under -ide:** side, ride, hide

Page 228 1. side; 2. day; 3. meet; 4. wide; 5. May; 6. feet

Page 229 1. ride, wide; 2. may, day; 3. meet, street; Answers will vary.

Page 230 1. today; 2. play; 3. sheet; 4. side; 5. hide

Page 232 1. beak; 2. fold; 3. seed; 4. gold; 5. weed; 6. peak; 7. feed; 8. hold

Page 233 **Beak:** leak, weak, peak, speak; **Gold:** bold, cold, fold, hold; **Seed:** need, weed, feed, bleed; 1. beak; 2. gold; 3. seed

Page 234 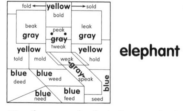 elephant

Under -eak: beak, peak, leak, tweak, weak, speak; **under -old:** fold, told, bold, sold, mold, hold; **under -eed:** seed, feed, weed, need, deed

Page 235 1. beak; 2. fold; 3. need; 4. weed; 5. hold; 6. feed

Page 236 1. speak, leak; 2. told, gold; 3. need, feed; Answers will vary.

Page 237 1. eat; 2. seed; 3. beak; 4. hold; 5. weeds; 6. needs